The Cycle of Foraging

~A Book of Days~

Written and Illustrated

by

Sean Wall

The Cycle of Foraging: A book of Days

Published by A Natural Place 2018

Copyright © Sean Wall

ISBN: 978-0692097960

Table of Contents

Acknowledgements

First and foremost, I need to thank my lovely wife and family, for enduring the mania that became the completion of this book. Without their support, and criticism at times, it would not have sprouted into the lovely work it has become. I would like to also thank all the interested individuals who pushed me to finish this book and have avidly awaited its release, your enthusiasm was the fuel that kept it going.

An Introduction

Note on Organization

The organization of this book came from a desire to provide as practical a source of information as possible. Many books and field guides have categorized plant species by flower shape and color, as well as plant type and even by habitat. However, the most common question I hear, is "what can I find growing outside to eat, right now?" This is a natural question, as foraging, like life in general, is a cycle. For someone just beginning to learn about edible wild plants, the amount of information available can be quite overwhelming. So, I wanted to provide interested parties with a dependable perspective; a reliable calendar that could be used to determine which natural resources where available, on any given day of the year.

The species presented in this book have been organized according to when their edible or useful parts become available throughout the year. This time frame has been divided up into months, or "moons", moving from the end of Winter, through Spring and Summer, into Fall and the return to Winter and rest. Each month has been described with a name and details of the natural events which are occurring during that specific time of year. Taken together then, a clear picture of how different natural events and processes fit together to form a cohesive whole can be gained.

The species contained herein can all be found across much of the Eastern United States, and the seasonal times described are accurate throughout much of the American Southeast, longitudinally from Texas to Georgia. As latitude increases North however, seasons for different species may be shifted forward by about a month, to account for the angle of the sun relative to the Earth, and the effect this will have on individual specie's life cycles. Specific regional variations may also occur, due to features of geography, nearby bodies of water, and soil type.

Considering the effects of different natural conditions, and the potential for variability across different species, this book may be used as a map, and a guide for reliably finding wild foods throughout the Natural environment, every month of the year. For this ability, it is not just a "book of days", but also a Book of Life.

Rules of Foraging

Gathering foods from the Wild can be both exhilarating and educational. However, there are a few important rules to remember whenever foraging. These can be summarized by 4 main points, all of which revolve around the concept of Respect:

- ❖ Respect for your body

- ❖ Respect for the species being harvested

- ❖ Respect for the local environment

- ❖ Respect for the law

First, and most importantly, no plant or wild food should be harvested unless 100% certainty of its identity is possible. Even if positive identification is more than likely, and there are no potentially dangerous plants similar to that specie which is being collected, the practice of never harvesting a plant unless it can be precisely identified is a most beneficial habit to form. Additionally, being mindful of the possibility of pollutants or other contamination when foraging, especially for aquatic species, is of utmost importance. Many aquatic, or wetland species will accumulate harmful chemicals in their bodies and roots, and those which may be compromised should not be harvested. Specimens which also grow alongside roadways, or other places where effluent or run-off from motor vehicles may collect should also be avoided.

Second, when harvesting from wild plants, it is important to be cognizant of the specie's presence and condition in the area. If a plant is not overly common, or actually quite rare, specimens of that plant should be left growing in most cases. Only when a plant occurs in large stands, or is otherwise common throughout a landscape, should the specie be readily harvested. However, should an uncommon specie be an excellent candidate for transplanting or propagation, the spreading of that specie can not only improve its local population and the greater ecosystem, but can also provide a more stable resource which may be utilized in the future.

This touches on the third important consideration when foraging; a specie's role or impact in the larger environment wherein it occurs. Many species have a beneficial impact on other forces and resources within an ecosystem and may play a vital role concerning species of wildlife as well. They may provide food and shelter, or mitigate erosion, or filter water sources and impact flooding and water retention. Simply put, some species of plant are important, and have an outsized impact on the environments in which they grow. When harvesting from these species, it is again important to consider their prevalence and proliferation before utilizing them.

Finally, it is advisable to respect human laws regarding private property before harvesting any specie. In nearly every instance, people are more than willing to allow what are commonly thought to be undesirable, or nuisance species to be removed from their properties. That being said, entering or crossing private properties without consent can result in legal fines and/or unnecessary confrontations, which can preclude positive community interactions in the future. In many cases, the interaction with private property owners is one of the best opportunities for educating the public regarding the wonderful natural resources our environment can provide us. It can also draw communities closer together in many cases too.

On Propagation

When propagating wild species of plants, there are essentially three different methods which are typically employed.

Either root or soft-wood cuttings may be taken in late Winter or early Spring and planted in prepared beds or large pots, depending on the specie. Rooting hormone, available at most nurseries and hardware stores may be applied in these instances, to ensure successful root development.

With some small, herbaceous species, transplanting of entire immature specimens can also be an option. Care must be taken when attempting to transplant any entire plant, however. It is important as little damage as possible is inflicted on the fragile root filaments, and that the specimen does not suffer from shock when placed in its new environment. Relocating a portion of the plant's original, or parent soil along with it can help to ensure similar nutrients are present in its new location. Also ensuring the plant is amply watered, and not placed in a drastically divergent habitat can greatly reduce the risk of detrimental shock. Seasonal timing is also important. Plants should not be transplanted once their flower buds have started to appear. Nor once the ambient temperatures become exceedingly hot during the day, typically around the beginning of May.

Propagation of ripe seeds is perhaps the easiest method for spreading of wild plants. The seeds must be scattered or planted immediately after they ripen, as they must endure a period of cold-hardening before they can successfully germinate the following Spring. In many species, failure to allow this can result in the seed entering a period of dormancy which can last for years. Because the weathering processes during the Winter months cause scattered seed to become buried by the soil on their own, care should also be taken not to plant wild seeds too deep, as the sun's rays may not reach them once Spring arrives.

A Forager's Perspective

My family has been foraging and utilizing wild species of edible plants for many years, and I have led many classes teaching people about foraging for wild foods, and in both instances, we have tried to cultivate and impart what may be termed the "Forager's Perspective", of Nature, life and our roles in the ecosystems we find ourselves in.

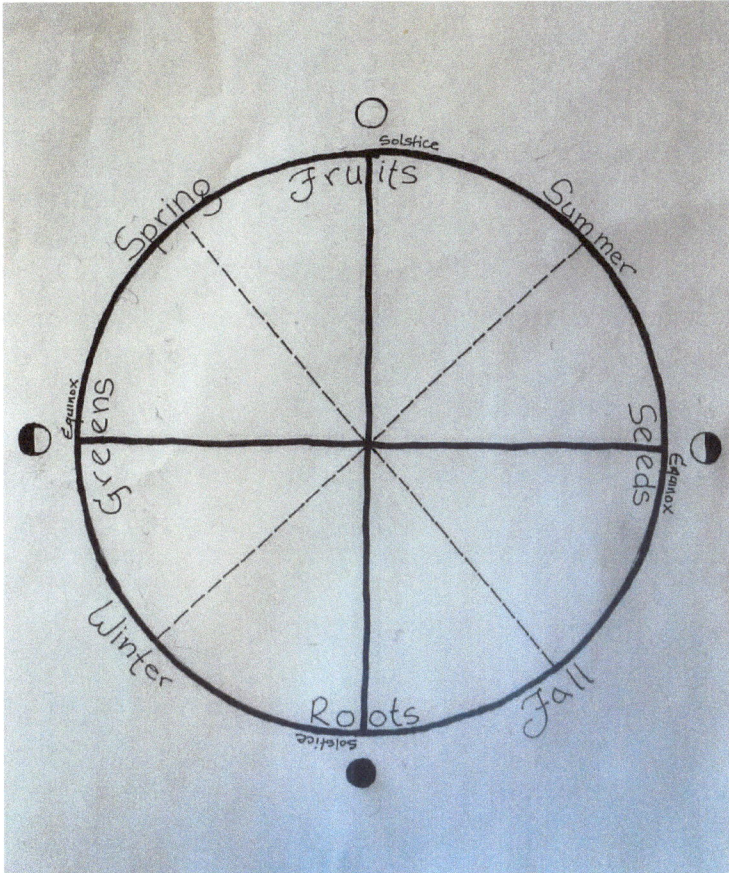

Life moves in a cycle throughout a landscape, and nowhere is this more apparent than in the local plant life. During the Spring, from March until June, most plants are producing new growth for the year or are growing into their adult, sexually-mature forms. During this time, an abundance of leafy greens and other vegetative parts can be found for harvesting. These resources are often the most packed with nutrition as plants are actively absorbing as many minerals as possible from the soil to strengthen their bodies and fuel their growth.

After the Spring storms and the Summer solstice pass though, at the end of June, this behavior changes. Most species are now ripening their fruits or blooming their flowers. The pattern of growth has shifted from focusing on personal development, to reproductive success and providing for future generations. After this shift occurs, the leafy, vegetative parts of most plants become more fibrous and less palatable. This is due to much of their available resources and fluids being redistributed to the reproductive organs. It is during these Summer months when we find delicious flowers, full of nectar and juicy, nutritious fruits hanging on both vine and tree. These fruits carry with them the promise of new generations and by the time late September and Fall arrive, even though the world wilts around them, these fruits will have gone to seed, ensuring the survival of their species for years to come.

Many of these seeds are some of the richest harvests available in the natural world, and as the weather turns cooler, their stored starches are transformed into simple sugars for helping them germinate the following Spring. Their offspring abroad in the world, most plants now either see an end to their lives, or else return to their roots and enter a state or dormancy for the coming Winter.

Though they may appear dormant however, the roots of perennial species are awake and busy during this time of year. The cold temperatures also activate the reserves of energy stored in these plants' roots, and they use the opportunity to stretch and grow, reaching and searching for new resources in the soil to help fuel their cycle of growth for the next year. During this season, these roots form the backbone of the forager's diet, as they are where much of the available life and energy are located.

It is important to notice how even in Winter, during the coldest part of the year, wild species are able to gain some form of advantage from these conditions; Winter is not without a purpose. This time of year affords them the opportunity to restore themselves, to reflect even, and grow stronger before the next growing season arrives.

This same cycle of life is not unique to species of plants either. From white-tailed deer, to songbirds, to little fish in Summer streams, all life follows a cycle of personal growth, communion, maturity, and rebirth. Knowing and understanding this pattern is not only extremely beneficial in helping to discover delicious species of wild edibles, it is an important tool in understanding the path and meaning of our own lives as well. It affords us the chance to grow personally very healthy, to build cohesive communities, and to find happiness. Most importantly though, it provides us with an enduring sense of hope.

That is the true Forager's Perspective.

We begin with the roots. Roots are always the beginning. By January the fiercest ice and snows and freezing temperatures arrive, forcing all life to take shelter and to hold onto what reserves of energy they have. The weather is also a catalyst however. Transforming those stores of energy into usable forms of sugars, it promotes the growth of new roots.

Without these harsh conditions, life could not return stronger year after year. The bitter cold kills everything back to their roots, but it allows us to tap into the latent energy found there, deep inside, bonding us together. A time of reflection and trial, but life always emerges stronger for the enduring of it.

The Moon of Ice

January

Canna lily (*Canna indica*)

The first plant we forage for at the beginning of each year is the luxuriant canna lily. Throughout the month of January, canna lilies are busy growing the networks of cream-colored roots which can make it a burden for traditional gardeners. Between the time of the Winter solstice and the beginning of February, these roots are full of delicious energy and are ripe for the picking. By March the plants have begun growing their new, great leaves for the year, and the sweet roots will turn more fibrous as their energy passes into the new foliage. The young, unfurled leaves can also be harvested as a leafy vegetable, but once the bright flowers appear in late Spring to early Summer, these too can become unpalatable. The flowers, and seeds which follow, are inedible, but their drying and desiccation in September signals that their roots are already beginning to store up energy for the Winter and will soon come into season again.

Canna lily is a semiaquatic family of plants with large, pointed, banana-like leaves, with an upright growing habitat and splays of beautiful yellow to red flowers. Capable of growing up to 6 feet tall, they can create quite an imposing presence where they are found. Their roots are highly adventitious, spreading rapidly through moist soils and crowding out most other species.

Native to the tropical and subtropical Americas, cannas are usually found in loose, well drained soils near water courses or in among wetland habitats. A sun-loving species, they are more often seen alongside slow moving, year-round streams rather than in deep, shaded swamps.

Canna roots have one of the highest starch contents of any plant and have been continuously harvested as a valuable food crop for thousands of years. The young roots are juicy and delicious and can be eaten raw or added to stir fries or other dishes as a cooked vegetable. Cooking the roots does help to caramelize the sugars present and further sweeten their flavor.

Canna lily plays an important role in mitigating erosion as well as providing shelter for a variety of wildlife species. They are also capable of improving water quality and as such can be indicators of overall wetland health. Cannas have become very popular as an ornamental garden species. They are hardy (even when not grown in a wetland!) and enjoy full sun. The flowers are important to a host of pollinator species and are a great way to attract beneficial wildlife to the area.

The most efficient method to grow canna is to transplant whole rootstock, or root cuttings during the Winter from existing specimens. As the roots are growing and full of energy during the Winter, it is the perfect time to propagate them to new locations. Cannas are highly adventitious; their roots will spread and clone very rapidly. One of the best, and delicious methods for keeping them in check, however, is to periodically harvest them during the Winter when they are trying to put out new roots.

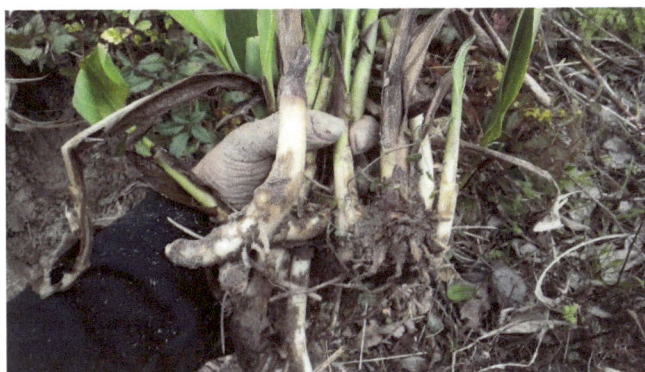

"If Winter comes,

    Can Spring be far behind?"

        -   Percy Bysshe Shelley, Ode to the West wind

We call this the Moon of Returning, not just because we see a return from seasonal migrations as far as wildlife are concerned. Nor rather for the return to blooming seen in floral species. During this moon, we start to see the first children of Spring; the redbud, the dogwood, and the thistle flower, the doves and the geese begin to return.

What we are really noticing though, is a return to intention, for both our bodies and our minds, to the pursuits for which they are developed. Whether that is returning to ancestral breeding grounds or simply to a more generative state of life, all living things are moving away from a state of dormancy, and so towards one of action.

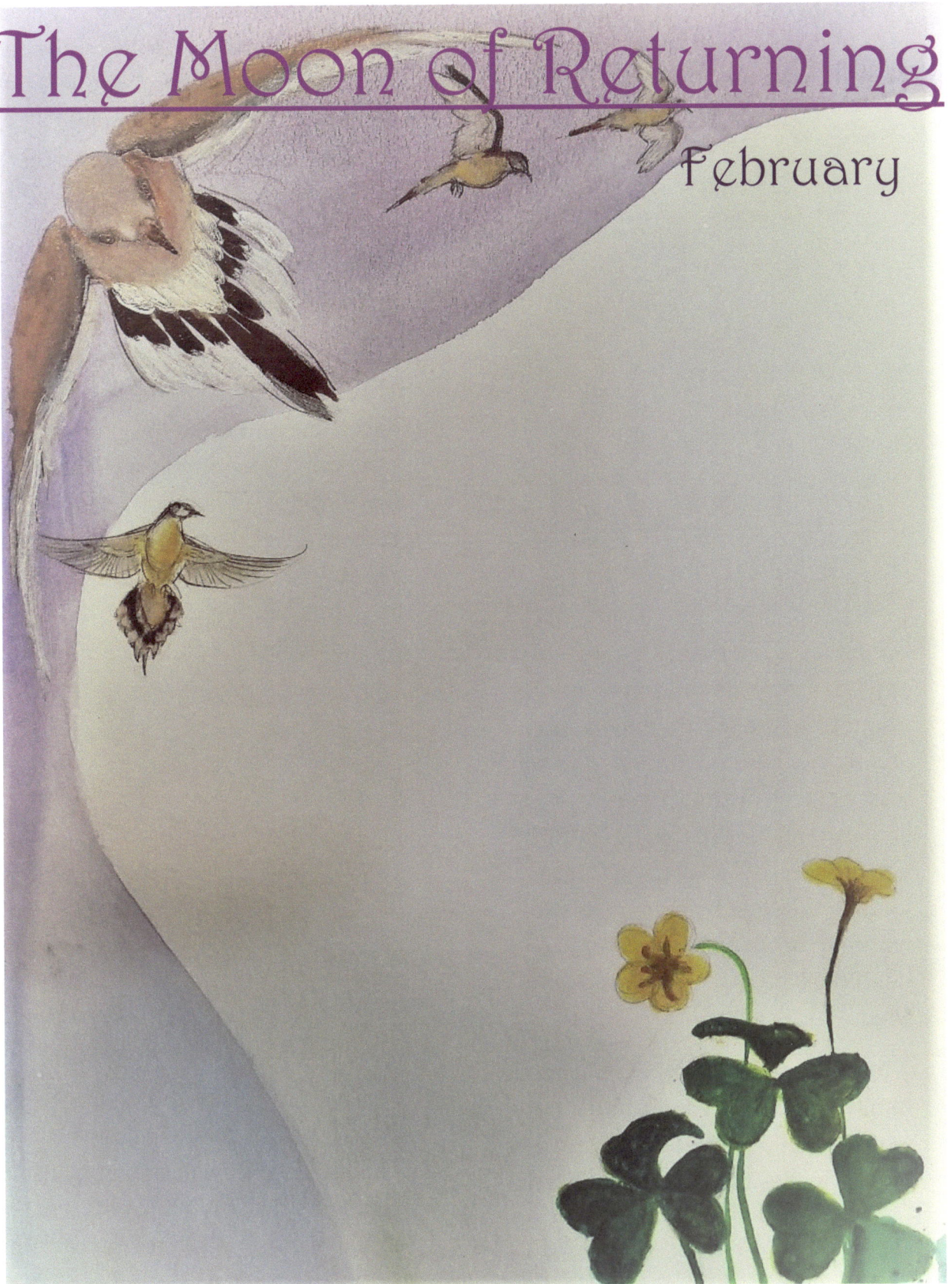

The Moon of Returning

February

Henbit (*Lamium amplxicaule*)

Henbit is another early leafy green to appear at the end of Winter. A member of the mint family, henbit generally shows up in yards and other waste places by the beginning of February and is capable of enduring late season cold snaps and freezes. In fact, by the time the sun begins to warm up other sleeping plants, henbit will have flowered and gone to seed.

A member of the mint, or *Lamiaceae* family, henbit is a small annual herb which usually grows to between 6 and 12 inches tall. Its straight, slender stem is square in cross-section and its leaves are rounded, deeply scalloped and oppositely arranged up its length. Further up its stem, the leaves become fused, clasping around the stem as a single blade. The small purple flowers emerge from the junctions of these fused leaves and are tubular in shape.

Preferring cool air and moisture, henbit is not overly fond of sheltered spaces, but rather stakes its claim out in the open. Henbit loves to form dense stands and is rarely seen growing alone. Look for it in open meadows or other open areas where the plants can feel the cold winds, while they last.

Every part of the henbit plant is edible raw, but the long stems become more fibrous as the plants age and begin producing flowers. The tender young heads and blooms are by far the best part to harvest and make a colorful addition to salads and their mild flavor can help to balance the taste of some other, more bitter, winter greens.

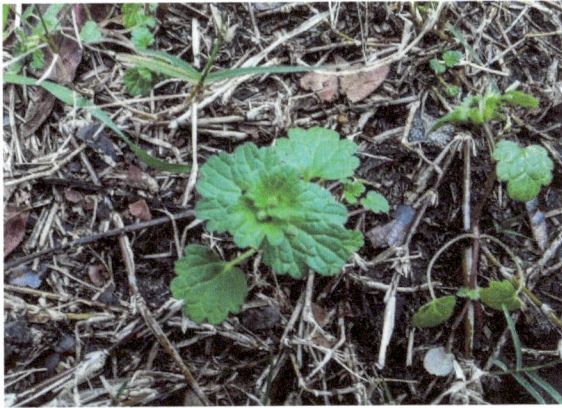

While considered by many to be weed, henbit flowers can provide an early spring source of nectar to long tongued bees, such as honey bees. The importance of nectar sources in late winter and early spring is of considerable importance to many pollinator species. As such an abundant species, it is hardly necessary to try and plant henbit, should you want to bring it into your garden or yard. Once some begins to grow on its own, it can be easily potted and moved to more desirable locations, either as forage for wildlife or as a potherb. Henbit can grow dense clumps but is a species small in stature and lacking the adventitious nature of many other wild species. Coupled with its relatively short

season, it is unlikely to dominate or take over any given locale.

Redbud (*Cercis canadensis*)

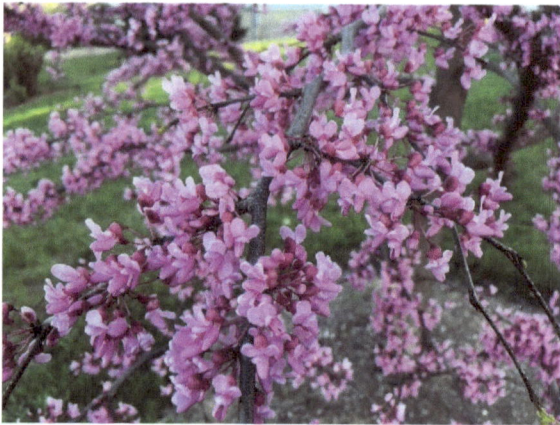

Redbud flowers are one of the harbingers of Spring. Along with dogwood trees, their bright blossoms stand out in stark contrast to the leafless, colorless and naked branches of the forest surrounding them. Beginning in early February, redbud blossoms begin to appear on the trees, before their leaves have sprouted for the year and about the same time that bird species start migrating back North from their wintering grounds in the South.

Redbud trees are small, rarely growing over 15 feet tall in the wild.

Their trunks are generally quite short and twisted while their limbs are thin and wispy. Their bark is dark and smooth but can become more scaly with age. Along with the bright pink flowers, the heart shaped leaves are very indicative of the specie. The flowers themselves are bright pink to magenta in color and appear in cluster along the branches, and the trunk too at times, several weeks before the leaves appear. The leaves are round, with a distinct heart shape. The fruit of the redbud tree is a small legume which forms about a month after the flowers appear and ripens by early to mid-April.

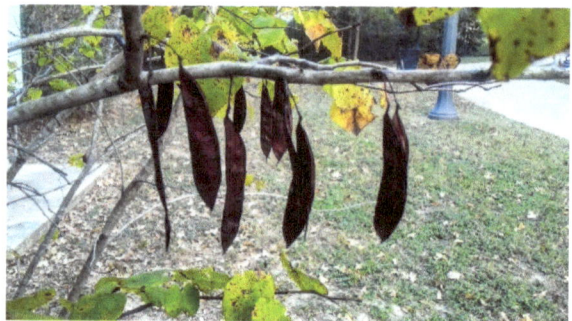

Redbud trees are a common understory tree in undisturbed woodlands. They prefer moist soils, however too much precipitation or flooding can be detrimental to them. Looking for them in late Winter, before other trees have bloomed is the best way to locate them in the wild; their characteristic flowers serve as a beacon in the otherwise dim, cold forests. Driving along wooded roads during this time of year, many redbud trees can be seen, especially near small creek crossings. Redbud trees are also very popular in landscaping; however, care should always be taken to obtain permission before harvesting from any species which may potentially lie on private property.

Redbud blooms are easy to collect, though the process may seem tedious because of their small size. Due to this it is encouraged to bring a group along to help make the experience more enjoyable. Care should be taken to ensure no single area of any one tree is totally denuded of blossoms however, as redbud trees are a vitally important to pollinator species. Redbud trees tend to flower en masse, so there is little danger of destroying their resource, but it is still important to

not take more than is needed. The buds and opened flowers have a delicate sweetness which makes them an absolute treat in early Spring salads or garnished on top of other dishes. The flowers are best fresh though and freezing them can cause them to lose some of their delicious, sweet flavor.

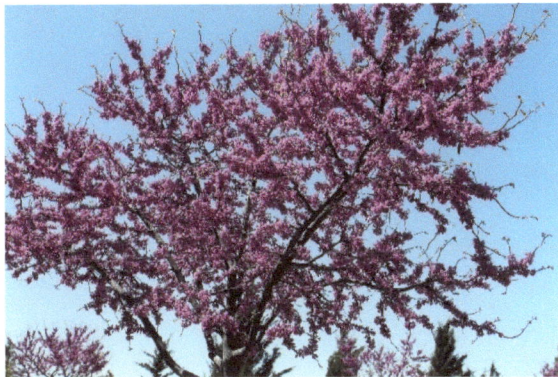

As has been stated, redbud flowers are an important food source for pollinator species that becomes available long before many others. Specialized bee species such as carpenter, or other long tongued bees, can take special advantage of the blooms. The leaves as well are an important food source for many different larval moths and butterflies. Larger wildlife species, such as white-tailed deer, will browse on the leaves, while several bird species including bobwhite quail will dine on the seeds. Propagation of most tree species is best accomplished by finding a reputable nursery in your local environment with healthy, young specimens available. However, as it is such a small specie, it is possible to transplant young individuals from the wild if great care is taken. Ensure as little damage as possible is done to the fine root follicles, and only transplant during the Winter, before temperatures start to rise, to avoid shocking the young tree.

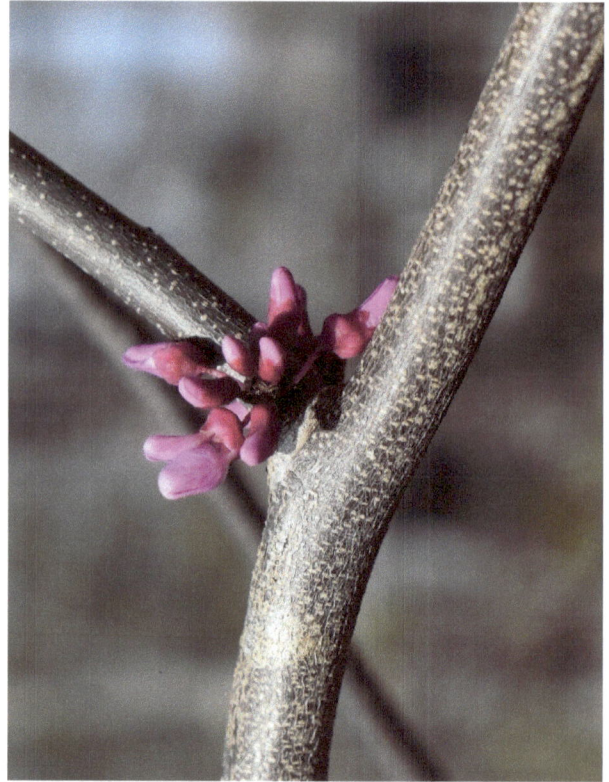

Wild Violet (*Viola spp.*)

Wild violets come into season from late February through the Spring equinox until April. They flower very early, any time between the end of February and the beginning of March. Once the flowers have bloomed however, the leaves and stems become drier and less palatable due to the plants transferring their available fluids and nutrients to their emerging blooms. They love and flourish in the cool but humid weather characteristic of the end of Winter and the beginning of Spring. By the time May comes and the Spring storms pass however, wild violets will have disappeared, replaced by other species in the yearly cycle of plant succession.

Violets are perennials which have heart shaped leaves with lightly scalloped margins which unfurl from a characteristic rolled up position as they sprout.

Wild violets are usually under 6 inches tall and each leaf extends on a thin, short stem from a central root bulb. Their flowers are small, five petaled and usually a faint cream to lavender color with a yellow center. The flowers form small, inconspicuous fruits by late Spring which pop open when ripe, scattering their seeds far and wide.

Similar to wood sorrel, wild violets prefer damp, shaded habitats with rich soils. They can even be found growing in or alongside areas which experience occasional flooding or high-water retention. Such soils provide ample nutrients to aid in the growth of the violets' root bulbs, ensuring their health for seasons to come.

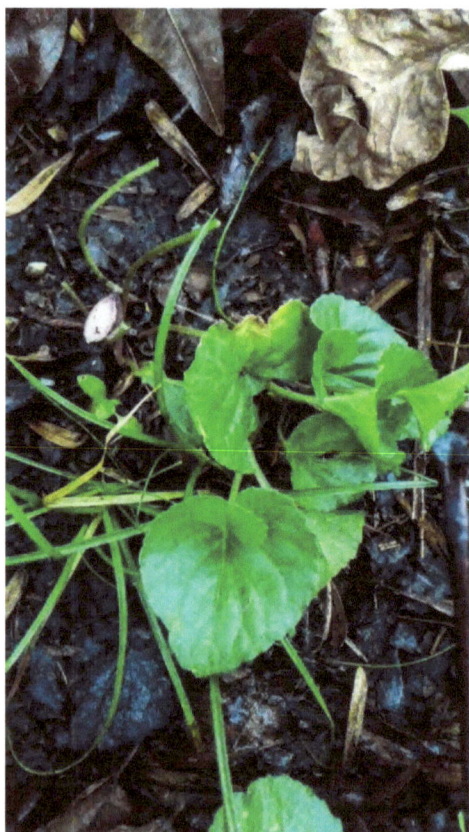

No special care is needed when harvesting or processing wild violet leaves. Like many leafy greens, they are edible raw, and several handfuls may be gathered on an early-Spring afternoon walk. Wild violets are a wonderful mild green, still rich in antioxidants and other nutrition. They make an excellent addition to salads or as a garnish or additive in other dishes.

Wild violets are an important source of food for a wide variety of wildlife. As one of the first nutritious greens to appear in the early Spring, they are an important source of vitamins and minerals for many animals after the long Winter. Pollinator species utilize their early blooming flowers as a source of nectar too. Caterpillars of several different moth and butterfly species also depend on their leaves for forage. Rabbits and other herbivores also occasionally browse on the tender, young greens. With these benefits in mind, wild violets are an easy species to transplant to new areas. Their central root bulbs are easily dug up with a trowel and, along with some of their parent soil, can be readily moved to pots or prepared beds outdoors. Once established, they will readily form small colonies which can return year after year.

Wood Sorrel (*Oxalis spp.*)

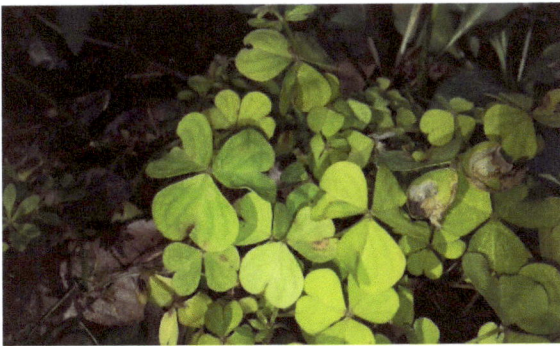

Wood sorrel is one of the first plants to emerge from Winter's chill, and in some sheltered areas it may even last all the year through actually. Their electric, lemony flavor is a bright ray of sunshine, while the world is still frozen and cold. The tartness is derived from oxalic acid which is present in the plant, so individuals with kidney problems, or other such concerns, may want to limit their intake to a few handfuls a week. In general, wood sorrel starts to produce new growth in the beginning of February, after the worst of the frosts have come, but still before things have really warmed up. With its triad of three heart shaped leaves, wood sorrel is unmistakable. The plants grow in clusters, emanating from a central root bulb. Their leaves can grow tiny (smaller than a penny) to huge (about the size of your palm).

Wood sorrel flowers are simple and five petaled, and can be either yellow or purple in color, depending on the sub-specie. Their fruits form by the beginning of May and resemble little green bananas, which also have a delicious, tart lemony flavor.

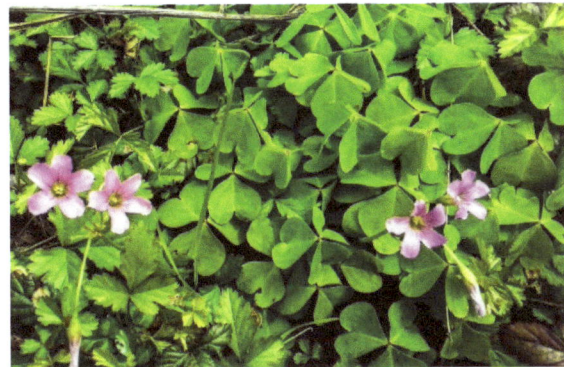

Wood sorrel can continue growing and popping up so long as there is ample moisture and the weather does not turn too hot or they are not too exposed. The best place to look for wood sorrel is in sheltered areas, under a forest canopy, or in little dells in a meadow; places where they can stay out of the dry wind and sun, but still get plenty of moisture. Areas that have deeper, richer soils are great for them as well. Wood sorrel is one of the more common plants, and small examples of it can even be found growing in your lawn or backyard.

If you find a large colony of wood sorrel, it is a simple matter to pick a great bagful, the same as if you were picking lettuce in your garden. Some restraint is always advised, but wood sorrel is a perennial that regrows larger every year from its central root bulb, and so if the roots are undisturbed, the plants will return each year. No special consideration is needed when preparing wood sorrel. The plant is delicious raw, and once the year heats up, it can be a refreshing treat on a hot day! Otherwise, they make surprising additions to salads or stir fry dishes.

Wood sorrel flowers are pollinated by a wide variety of native bees and other pollinators such as wasps and yellow-jackets, but also a plethora of butterflies as well. These early blooming flowers can be very helpful to pollinator species looking for nectar before most other plant species have bloomed. Planting them in pots or around your garden can be very beneficial to these species and help to improve the micro-habitat of your home but can also provide a delicious wild treat. The easiest and best way to start a new wood sorrel colony is to transplant a cluster of

root bulbs in late Winter or early Spring, before they have begun growing in earnest. Once they are established, they will begin propagating themselves readily by seed as well.

Cleavers (*Galium aparine*)

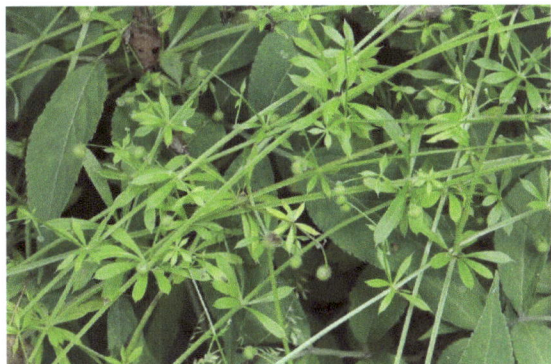

Cleavers appear just as the coldest parts of Winter come; usually around mid to late February. The first of many cold loving greens to appear, cleavers are a herald of sorts to the coming of Spring; the bright lime green of their bodies standing in stark contrast to the frigid brown of the dormant forest floor. Once March ends and the weather starts to heat up, the plants will have bloomed their small, white flowers and gone to seed however.

Cleavers have long, thin trailing bodies which produce 5 – 7 leaflets in a whorl around their stem. The stem is covered in tiny, fine hairs which give it a clinging habit. The small flowers are white, 5-petaled, and very tiny. The small, green seeds which follow are also covered in the same fine hairs as the stem, ensuring they are able to travel far and wide as they cling to anything which passes by.

Cleavers typically appear along fence lines or along the edge of the forest, the structure of these places lending them both support for their thin stems and access to sunlight without over-exposing them. Cleavers enjoy crisp, moist environments and higher temperatures or too much sunlight can leave them dried out and desiccated. Their trailing, clinging stems can form dense mats of vegetation if left unchecked.

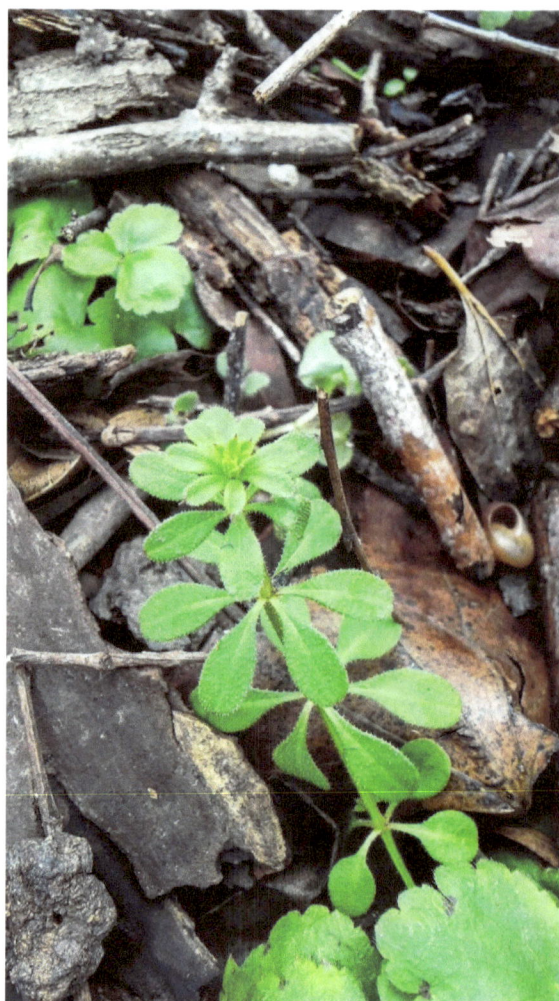

Cleavers are best harvested when young and immature. Typically, those which are under 6 inches in height are the most delicious, as they have not become overly hairy or fibrous. They are a great addition to early Spring salads or as a cooked vegetable. The wonderful tea for which cleaver is known, can be made with plants of any age however. Taken with honey, it is an excellent source of vitamin C, at a time of year when seasonal colds are all too common a malady.

Cleavers are an exceptionally common plant, and in most cases, need not be managed for, as they will appear on their own. Should they be desired as a pot herb however, the ripened seeds of mature plants can be collected and sprouted, either indoors or outside in prepared beds.

Stinging nettle (*Urtica dioica*)

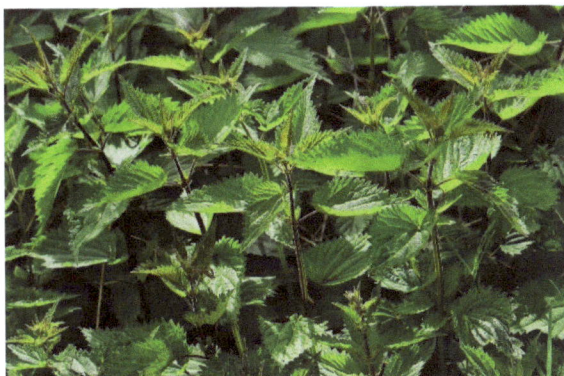

Stinging nettles sprout at the same time of year as wild violets or wood sorrel, and usually enjoy the same type of environment as well. The cool, crisp weather at the end of Winter, before Spring has truly begun, is perfect for them. Yet by the end of Spring, in May or June, they have been replaced by other species more tolerant of higher temperatures.

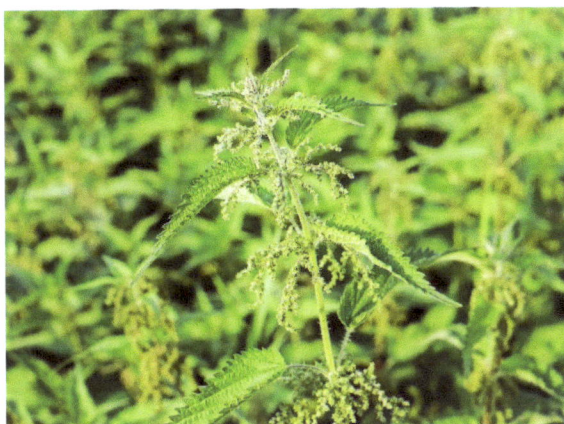

Stinging nettle is a low growing, perennial herb which, as the name implies, is covered in tiny, hollow stinging hairs. Its pointed, soft green leaves are serrated, highly vascularized and appear oppositely up its wiry stem. Being dioecious, both male and female plants exist, and their unassuming flowers can range in color from yellow or green to purple or brown. The roots of the species send out fast growing rhizomes which will sprout new plants along their length, in addition to those sprouted from seed.

Stinging nettles love to grow in cool, damp environments, in soils with a decent amount of organic matter. This is much the same habitat preferred by wild violets and wood sorrel both, however the three will rarely ever be seen growing together in the wild.

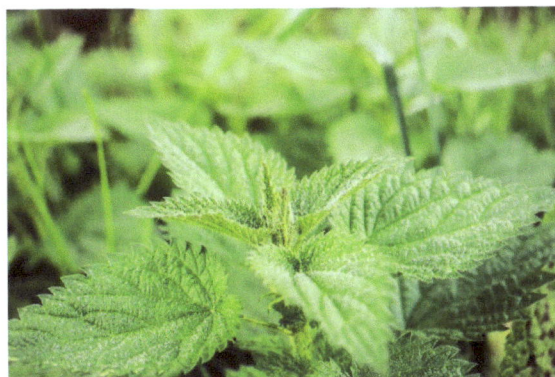

Great care should be taken when harvesting stinging nettles to avoid the stinging hairs. Thick gloves should be worn when handling the raw plants and once harvested, they should be boiled for a minimum of 10

– 12 minutes to remove the hairs and the chemicals inside. Stinging nettle has a long history as a cooked vegetable and is well known for its high nutrition. It is rich in vitamins A and C, as well as other important minerals such as iron and calcium. The cooked greens may be served with sautéed garlic or in stir fry dishes with nuts or seeds. The infused water from cooking them is also a delicious and healthy beverage that can be enjoyed as an herbal tea.

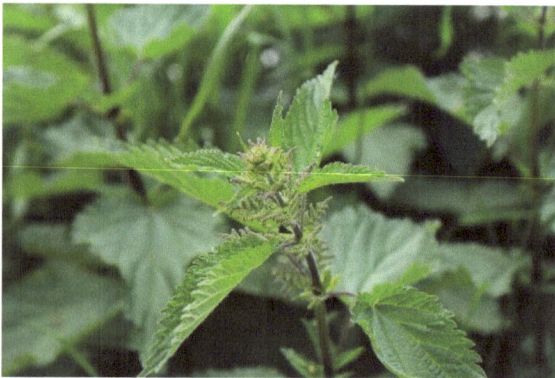

The larvae of several different moth and butterfly species depend on the foliage of stinging nettles for food, some almost exclusively. Larger herbivores tend to avoid the plant however, due to the presence of the hypodermic hairs. Should propagation of stinging nettles be desired, young plants can be transplanted before the flower buds appear. Root cuttings can also be taken and sprouted in pots or prepared outdoor beds. Due to the adventitious nature of their roots, stinging nettles can form dense colonies which may crowd out other, desired species. Their stinging hairs can make these groups seem intimidating, but as with many adventitious species, the best method of control is to harvest and eat them.

Chickweed (*Stellaria media*)

Another late Winter, early Spring green, chickweed begins growing in early to mid-February, just after the chill of Winter starts to thaw. It takes advantage of the cool, moist temperatures, as too much warm sunlight can hinder its growth or cause it to be crowded out by taller-growing species. In ideal habitats though, it can still be found growing much later in the year. However, by mid-March, its small flowers will have bloomed and its leaves and stems subsequently turned fibrous and dry.

Chickweed is an annual, small, cold weather plant that does not usually grow above 6 inches tall. Its short, pinnate leaves are oppositely arranged up its stem with its small, simple flowers blooming from between its two topmost leaves. The flowers are usually white, but can also be yellow, with an average of 10 thin petals arrayed around its center. As a ground cover species, chickweed can form thick mats where it grows,

similar to many species of clover or other low growing, herbaceous species.

Chickweed prefers cool, shaded spots to grow and spread in. As a late Winter plant, areas where it can stay moist, but not overly warm, are good places to see it still thriving later in the year. Spots under larger, overarching trees or in damp spots along the edges of woodlands where it is overly dense and humid are ideal places to see chickweed growing. Out of full sunlight, the greatest inhibitor of chickweed's growth is competition from taller, fast growing species which can crowd it out.

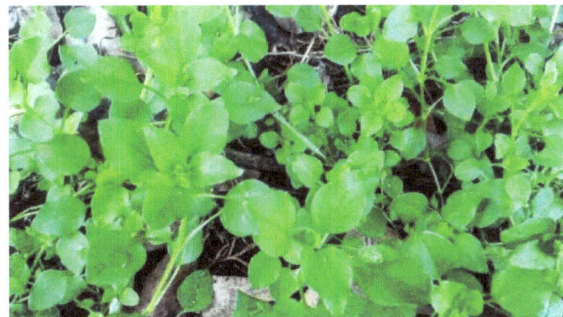

Harvesting chickweed, like many greens, is very simple. Plucking the tops of plants off when foraging allows the remainder of the plant to continue growing, and possibly still reproduce. The topmost portion of the plant will also be the youngest and most tender as well. Since chickweed grows in such abundance when in season, there is little danger of over harvesting the specie where it is found. The leaves are good raw in late Winter, early Spring salads. They are a relatively mild green and so are perfect for mixing with more bitter greens like dandelions or wild lettuce. They may also be boiled as with spinach leaves and served as a cooked vegetable or as an addition to other dishes.

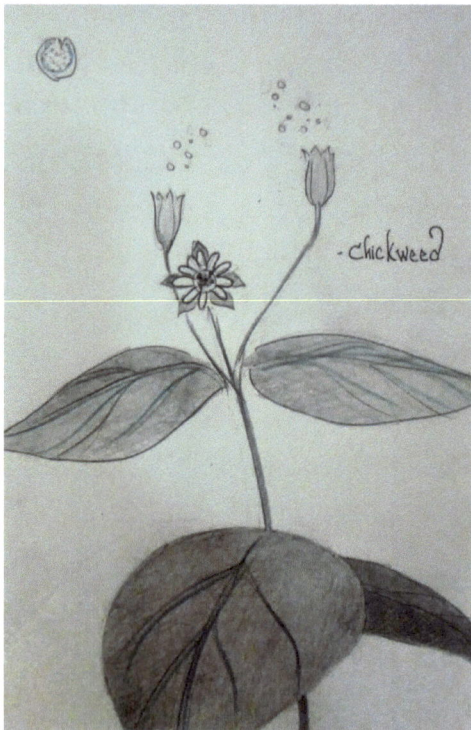

- chickweed

As a ground cover, chickweed can help to secure soils which would otherwise be lost to erosion, especially once the Spring rains begin in late March to early April. It is also visited by several species of Spring pollinators as a source of nectar before many species of wildflower have begun blooming. The leaves themselves are also foraged for by several different wildlife species, including white-tailed deer, rabbits, and the larval forms of many pollinator species. Propagation of chickweed can follow one of two methods. Very young seedlings can be gently transplanted to prepared beds or pots, or the small, ripe seeds may be carefully collected and planted. As always, it is a good idea to utilize some of the plant's parent soil when transplanting to a new location. The soils a particular plant, or seed, is adapted to will contain all of the minerals the individual plant has become accustomed to and can help to help ensure a similar chemical consistency and avoid shock to the roots as well as promote successful germination. Chickweed is an extremely common species, and in many cases, given the proper environment, will simply show up on its own. Should this happen in an outdoor bed where the plant is desired, all that is left to do is let it grow and flourish.

Wine Cups (*Callirhoe involucrata*)

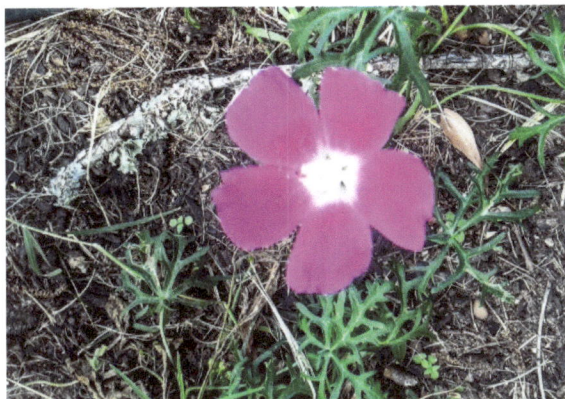

Wine cups begin growing almost as soon as the last freeze of Winter has passed, but are hard to notice before their long, spindly leaves and vibrant flowers reach above the level of the dry grasses around them. From the end of January to the middle of March, the roots of the wine cup plant are still full of sweet starches and are a delicious harvest. By the end of March and into April, the bright flowers begin to appear, and the roots become decidedly more fibrous. The plants quickly go to seed afterwards, however several generations of the plants can be seen sprouting during a single year.

Wine cups are a slightly more difficult plant to identify for beginners. Due to its growing habit with long trailing stems and thin, palmate leaves, it can be hard to notice and still more difficult to follow the stems back to the central taproot. They typically produce 5 – 7 long, trailing stems which terminate in a single, thin, palmate leaf. These stems can be up to 1-foot long. The flowers which appear later are pink to deep purple in color and 5-petaled. The bright, magenta flowers for which they are named are the best way to identify the plants, but at this point, the roots usually have become too fibrous to be enjoyable.

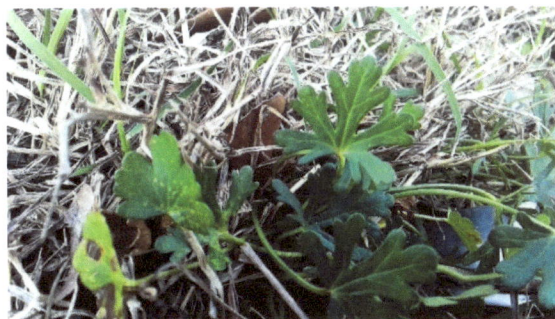

Wine cups love and flourish best in open meadows and prairies, and the presence of grasses or other forbs can make picking them out hard. They are also quite fond of people's gardens and flower beds, though. When growing among your yard they can be much easier to identify, as grasses are usually kept to a minimum and the plants are easier to spot.

When harvesting wine cups, removing the entire tap root can prove difficult. Wine cup tap roots can be up to 6 inches long, and clay-rich prairie soils can make their removal difficult. Locating the species when in season can also be tricky, however wine cups do typically grow in colonies though and can be counted on to come back in the same place year after year. As such, once a stand is identified, they can be relocated earlier the following year when the tender roots are still in season. Wine cup roots have a flavor similar to water chestnut and a texture much like domestic carrots. They are best eaten raw and fresh, though, as cooking can overly dry them out.

Wine cup flowers are important for pollinator species, and the plant does play its part in securing topsoil, but not much eats the large taproots, besides humans. Early in spring to late winter before the flowers appear, the roots are best, but can still be difficult to find. Flowers make identification easier, but the roots may be more fibrous by then. The best method for propagation is to transplant whole roots, usually before the flowers appear in late winter, or in Fall after the stems begin to wither.

Curly Dock (*Rumex crispus*)

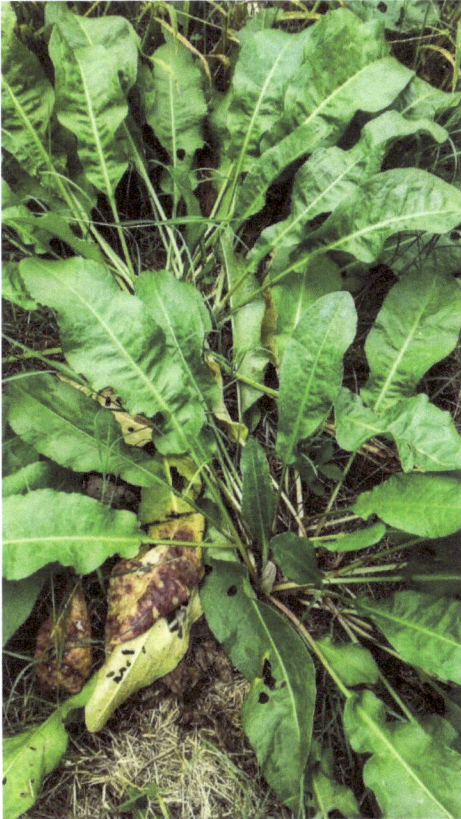

Like some other late Winter, early Spring greens, curly (or yellow) dock has an indeterminate growth; it will continue growing throughout the year provided conditions are amenable. On average though, it begins its life cycle starting in mid to late February, as daylight hours start to increase with the advent of the Spring equinox and warmer weather. After Spring begins, it produces its central stalk and begins ripening the seeds which form along its length. Any time there is a rain shower, followed by warm,

sunny weather, dock plants will begin producing new growth. So its lush, broad leaves may be harvested year-round.

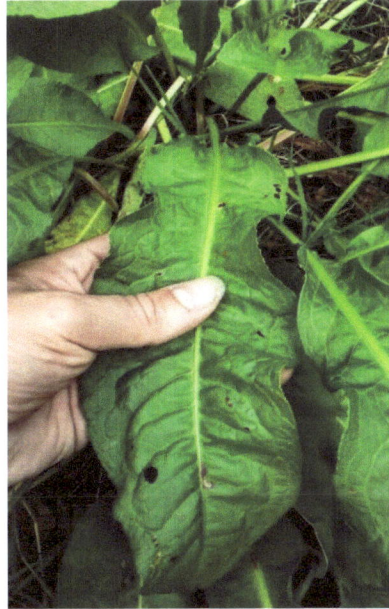

Curly dock is a low growing, leafy green which forms a large basal rosette. A hollow, fibrous stalk, 2 – 3 feet tall, grows out of the middle of the rosette which bears the dense clusters of flowers and seeds. The leaves of the curly dock plant are broad and long, with a large central rib, and a characteristic wavy margin. Young leaves start off ovoid and smooth along their margins, extending singularly up from the ground on long, thin stems. As they age, dock leaves may become darker and rougher in texture, however they still remain an excellent source of nutrition.

which can become more concentrated as the plant ages. These acids are not present in dangerous quantities and exist in many varieties of store-bought vegetables as well. However, individuals who experience problems related to kidney stones, or other kidney-related issues should consult their physician before consuming oxalate bearing species or avoid consuming them in large amounts.

- Curly Dock

Curly dock leaves are easy to harvest and grow in such abundance that a good harvest is usually assured without risking damage to the plants' population. Younger leaves are delicious raw, added to salads or as a vegetable in other dishes. More mature leaves are better suited to cooking, either served as a side like spinach or in soups or stews, or in stir fried dishes as well. Curly dock leaves have a mild, somewhat tart flavor, due to the presence of oxalic acids,

Bastard Cabbage (*Rapistrum rugostrum*)

Bastard cabbage usually appears in February, after any late-Winter rains which are followed by warmer, mild sunny weather. They grow very rapidly, and after flowering in March or April, they quickly go to seed. Before May, their large, luxuriant leaves have disappeared from the landscape due to the rising temperatures, replaced by large stands of grass. Similar to curly dock though, once the weather cools, they may return at any time, provided amenable conditions are present.

A member of the *Brassicaceae* family, bastard cabbage is a mustard species which produces large, wide leaves with wavy, lobed margins. They have blunt, rounded tips and a large, central rib as well. These leaves form large basal rosettes, often several feet in diameter. Their small, simple flowers are light yellow in color and appear in bunches on the end of long, branched stems emanating from a tall central stalk, which grows up from their base. The species can either appear as an annual, or in good conditions as a biennial with a two-year life cycle, waiting until its second year to reach maturity and produce its flower bearing stalk.

Bastard cabbages are common sights along roadside is early Spring, or late winter, and fare best in sunny meadows or open fields. In areas that retain moisture or border small streams, the species may be seen to linger into late Spring, early Summer, as they are less affected by increasing temperatures and competition from other species.

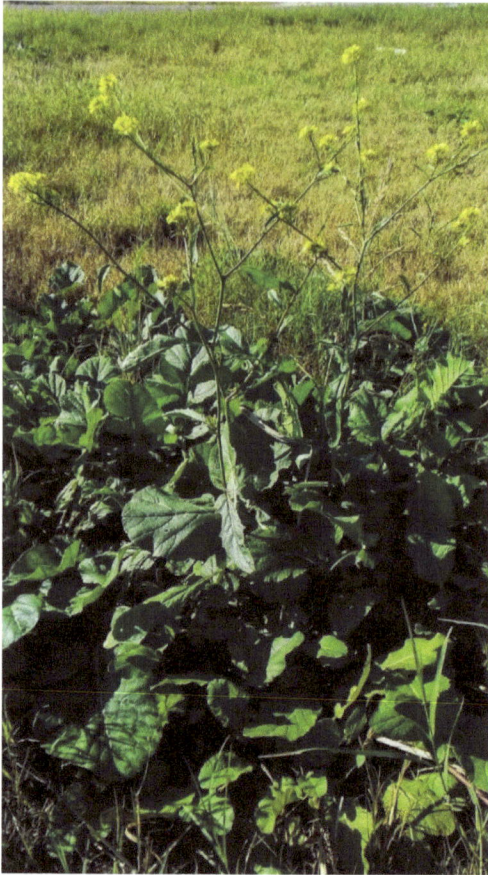

Like many other *Brassicaceae* species, bastard cabbage does well as a cooked green. Its leaves may be enjoyed raw, in salad, if they are picked when immature, before they are over 6 – 7 inches long and the flowers appear on the plant. More mature leaves are better cooked, as they become more bitter once the plant begins redirecting its fluids, minerals and energy towards its reproductive structures. Harvesting the leaves themselves is as simple as

with many other leafy green species and several bags may be filled in a short time span. Bastard cabbage usually grows in large groups, and there is such an abundance of them when in season that there is little chance of damaging their local populations.

Flowers of the bastard cabbage are utilized by pollinator species, and like many members of the mustard family, its large leaves are an important food source for many herbivorous wildlife species too. An easy plant to grow, ripened seed pods may be collected and planted in desired locations. However, it may be easier to pot and transplant young individuals to prepared beds from the wild. This should be done as soon as the plants emerge, either in late December or January, depending on the weather. This specie flowers rather early, and once it does so, it can be detrimental to the plant to attempt to move it.

The month we term the Moon of Eggs is the month wherein Spring truly begins. Many species of migratory birds have already returned from the South and started building their nests and laying their eggs. Likewise, most species of flowering plants have begun growing young buds which will eventually blossom into a new and beautiful generation themselves. This time of year has traditionally been seen as a time of new beginnings and rebirth, both personally and in terms of the greater natural environment.

Additionally, the image of the egg has been a symbol for this transformative process in many cultures as well. The year is in incubation, with so many possibilities or pitfalls waiting ahead. By the same token, our goals and aspirations for the new year are forming, waiting to hatch too. At this moment, they are perfect in their possibilities, but once they start to bloom, they will need nurturing and dedication in order to reach their full potential - like all living things.

The Moon of Eggs

March

Silverberry (*Eleagnus spp.*)

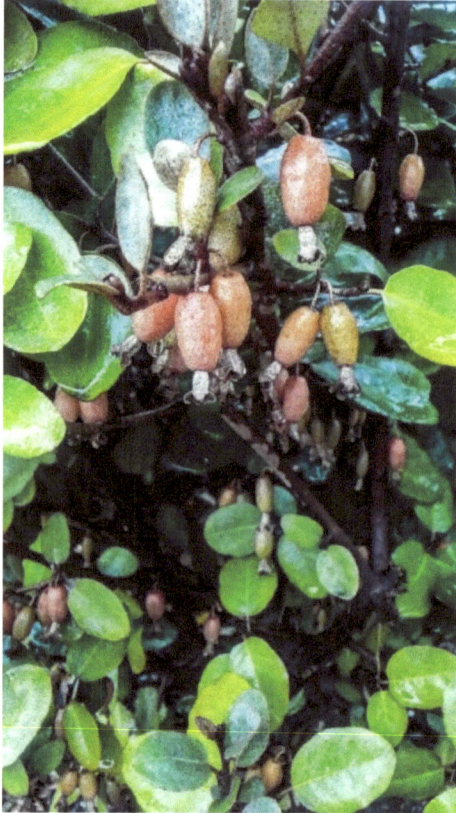

Silverberry is unique in that it is the only fruiting species available before the month of May. The fragrant flowers of *Eleagnus*, or silverberry, species bloom incredibly early, sometimes as early as the beginning of January and the fruits will begin ripening by the end of February.

A low to middle height shrub, silverberry generally grows to between 4 – 6 feet tall. Its broad, lanceolate leaves are light green with a mottled, silvery texture. Silverberry flowers are small, but very fragrant

and usually buzzing with pollinator species. The resultant fruits start off a light brown color with the same silvery texture, but ripen to a bright red. The fruits are ovate and about 1 inch in length. A single, edible seed is present in the center of each fruit.

Silverberries prefer to grow in well drained, sandy or gravely soils, either in meadow uplands or along forest edges. Naturally a drier climate plant, it can still thrive in humid or moist soils, provided its roots are not continuously inundated with standing water. Silverberry is a popular species in both residential and commercial landscaping and so can be found in a variety of urban environments. Permission is always important before collecting from private property, but the areas around properties where silverberry has been planted can be ideal places to look for feral individuals as well.

To harvest silverberry, wait until the berries turn bright red. At first, while they are a silver-flecked brown, they are rather astringent. Once they are ripe however, collecting as any other berry in buckets is as good a method as any. Silverberries are wonderfully delicious. The seeds are high in essential fatty acids as well; an important source of nutrition not usually seen in plants. The fruit of the berry is pulpy and the large seed in the middle is delicately crunchy. The seed may be discarded or eaten along with the rest of the fruit. The fruit can be used as many other berries; in jams or jellies, as a topping for desserts, or plain - fresh off the vine.

Silverberry flowers are doubly beneficial to wildlife; they are an early source of nectar, long before any other species have bloomed, and their fruits are a source of calories and sugars in a time when forage is hard to find for many species. Propagation of silverberry bushes can be achieved by taking root stock cuttings during early Winter, usually around late December. Because silverberry blooms so early, waiting until January or February could find the plant already beginning its new growth cycle for the year. Finding a reputable nursery in your same plant hardiness zone, with healthy native varieties, is another good option always worth considering when thinking of planting woody species.

Wild Onion (*Allium spp.*)

The last, and perhaps greatest, of the roots to be gathered, wild onions come into season by mid-March. Their thin, succulent stems can begin sprouting up by early February, but they are easily lost in the grasses around them until their immature flower heads emerge in late March to early April. Their flowers bloom throughout April and into May, but by June and Midsummer, they will have disappeared until the following Spring.

Wild onion is easily recognizable, by its signature smell if nothing else. Its bulbs can be anywhere between ½ to 3 inches across. Their leaves are typically 1 inch or less thick and decidedly more succulent in appearance than the emergent grasses around them. Their flowers are small, white to purple in color and 5-petaled. They appear on the ends of thin, short stalks branching from a central stem rising from the midst of their base. Their seeds are fleshy and egg-shaped, being no larger than the average pea.

Wild onion typically grows in large bunches - sometimes spread across entire meadows. They are fond of full to partial shade and rich, well drained soils which receive plenty of moisture. They are often seen along the banks of small creeks which may experience seasonal inundation. Occasionally they may be found in such areas amongst woodlands, but more often they are seen growing in the open, across water meadows or along sunny streams.

When harvesting wild onion, it can prove difficult, depending on the soils, to remove the entire root bulb. The whole plant is edible however, and the portion of root left behind can sprout a new plant the following year. Wild onions can be used similar to any domestic onion. They are wonderful cooked in soups or other dishes, or even raw in salads.

Wild onion flowers are attractive to pollinators, however not many other species of wildlife make use of the plant for food. The large stands of them along waterways, or other flood-prone areas, can help to

mitigate the effects of erosion though. Propagation of the species is similar to wine cups; transplanting whole, immature plants to new locations, before the flowers have emerged. However, wild onions do sprout readily from seed, and gathering and planting the ripe seeds in late April or May can be effective.

Dandelion (*Taraxacum officinale*)

The perennial dandelion is perhaps one of the better known wild edibles. It appears in the early Spring, usually popping up in March. Its characteristic yellow flowers can be seen in large groups spread across lawns and other open areas. By May, its yellow flower heads have been pollinated and turned into the famous seed heads which people are so fond of. These seeds are wind dispersed of course, and it is due to their airborne agility that dandelions are capable of spreading so far and wide.

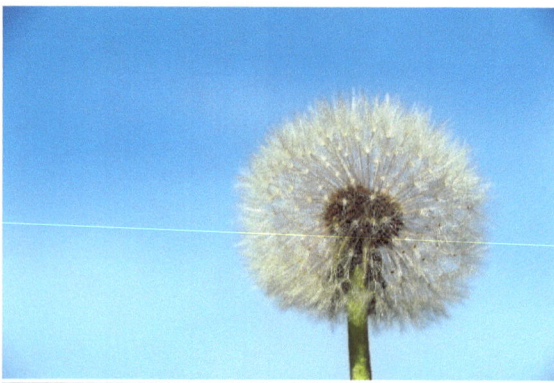

Dandelion is a relatively small, perennial herbaceous plant which sprouts every year from a large central taproot. Its characteristic leaves are deeply toothed, giving rise to its common name; "Dent-de-Leon", "lion's teeth". These easily recognizable leaves form a low basal rosette, from which the central flower stalk later appears. The stalk is thin and hollow, bearing a single flower in two stages. The flowers first bloom bright yellow, with many simple rays, and then close upon pollination. When they next re-open, it is as the white, fluffy seed-heads for which they are best known.

Dandelion can be found equally in both sheltered and open, sunny areas. A common sight in both manicured lawns and waste areas, dandelion is perhaps one of the most prolific of wild edibles, and as such is one of the best well known. Ever the re-colonizer, it seems to love growing in the cracks of sidewalks or in any place in which it might be unwelcome. However, it is in the more sheltered, moist locations that dandelions will grow to their largest size.

The large-toothed leaves of the dandelion are a nutritious leafy green but can be somewhat bitter. They are best enjoyed cooked or mixed with other, more mild greens to dilute their strong flavor. The yellow flowers are edible as well and can either be mixed into salads or even be processed into a delicious dandelion wine.

Dandelion nectar is an important food source for a wide variety of pollinator species during the early spring before many other species have flowered. The honey bee in particular depends on the arrival of dandelion flowers in the early spring to ensure a sufficient food supply.

Like many spring greens, dandelion is best transplanted once it appears in any location via potting into small pots and growing either in a prepared bed, as a potherb or really in any outdoor location.

Wild Lettuce (*Lactuca spp.*)

Like many species in the *Asteraceae* family, wild lettuces first begin to grow as low rosettes in early March. However, they quickly can grow to tall heights and by May can be well over 4 feet tall. By this time they usually have gone to seed, and shortly whither back to their roots.

Wild lettuce has a growth habit very similar to both dandelion and many wild thistle species. Beginning with the formation of a basal rosette, the plant then sends up a tall central stalk which terminates in its flower-bearing parts. Each of its leaves are sharply toothed, but the ends are decidedly more rounded. A prominent rib runs along the underside of each leaf, and in some varieties this rib may exhibit fine hairs or spines. The apex of the plant can reach heights of up 9 feet tall but is more commonly seen at 3 – 6 feet, depending on habitat and conditions. Its flowers are produced similarly to sow thistle, in that several may be produced on thin, branched stems. These flowers also develop in 2 distinct stages, with a white, fluffy seed-head culminating the second stage. Once the seeds are dispersed, the plant dies back to its large, central taproot, storing up energy and resources for the next growing season.

Like dandelion, wild lettuce does equally well in either sunny or shaded locations but is usually allowed to grow to its prodigious heights in more out of the way areas, such as within forest margins. Looking just inside the edge of a forest in April, you can typically find one of these large plants growing upwards of 3 feet tall already.

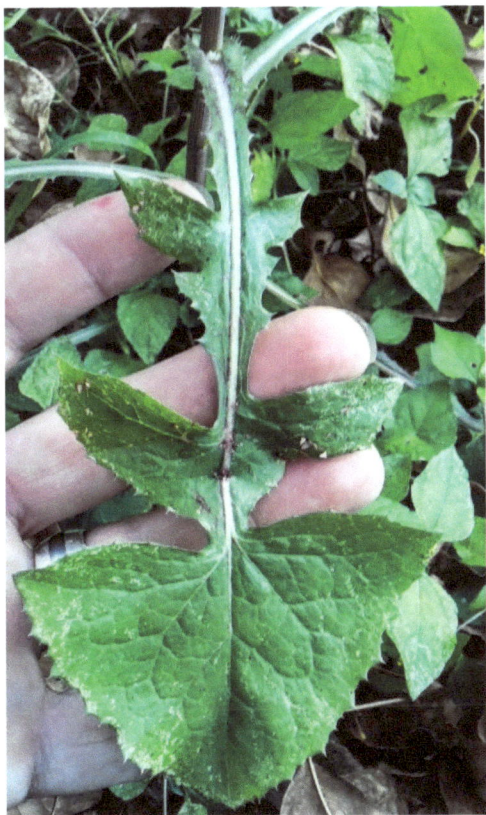

There are two species of wild lettuce which grow here: *L. serriola* and *L. canadensis*. Of the two, *canadensis* is the much more palatable species, as *serriola* produces a small ridge of spines along the underside of each leaf. Both species are still well enjoyed as a cooked green however, while *canadensis* also makes a great addition to salads. As the specie grows, it is the youngest leaves, nearest the top, which are the best to harvest. So, allowing the plants to continue growing ensures a prolonged selection of new leaves to choose from.

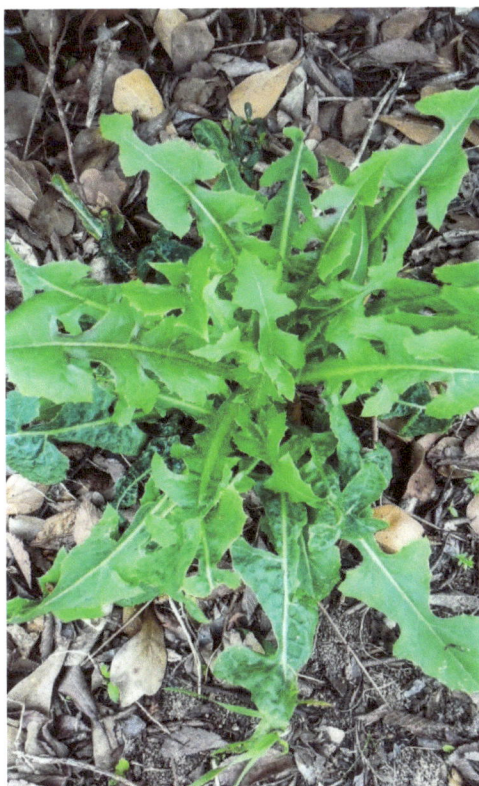

Just as with dandelions and other early spring bloomers, wild lettuce flowers are an important source of nectar to pollinators, especially bees. They can be readily transplanted while still in their basal rosette stage, but due to their tall growing habit, they make poor choices for keeping in pots. They do well planted along the edge of beds as a margin or in other sheltered areas where they can grow to their full height, providing a continued source of nutritious greens, and help to attract pollinators to your area.

Spring Equinox

"Following Winter's strife, a warm air rises,

teemed with Life.

Birth, re-birth as the waiting die.

Old love, new love, sprouts wings to fly."

-Phar West Nagle

The sunny, but cool idyllic days of March give way to the dark and drenching rains of April. Though the storms may seem intimidating, they are perhaps one of the greatest opportunities for growth throughout the year. The sudden influx of so much precipitation, and with it so many effluvial minerals and nutrients, serves as a catalyst to the multitudes of nascent life forms, just waiting to burst forth.

Often it is the dark and even daunting times which challenge us and push us to reach new heights. While they can force us to abandon or let go of goals or paths which we are intent on, they also provide the opportunity for new experiences and ideas we may not have encountered otherwise. Just as these seasonal floods can wash away much of what we may hold dear, more importantly they also bring opportunities for change and provide the sustenance necessary for life.

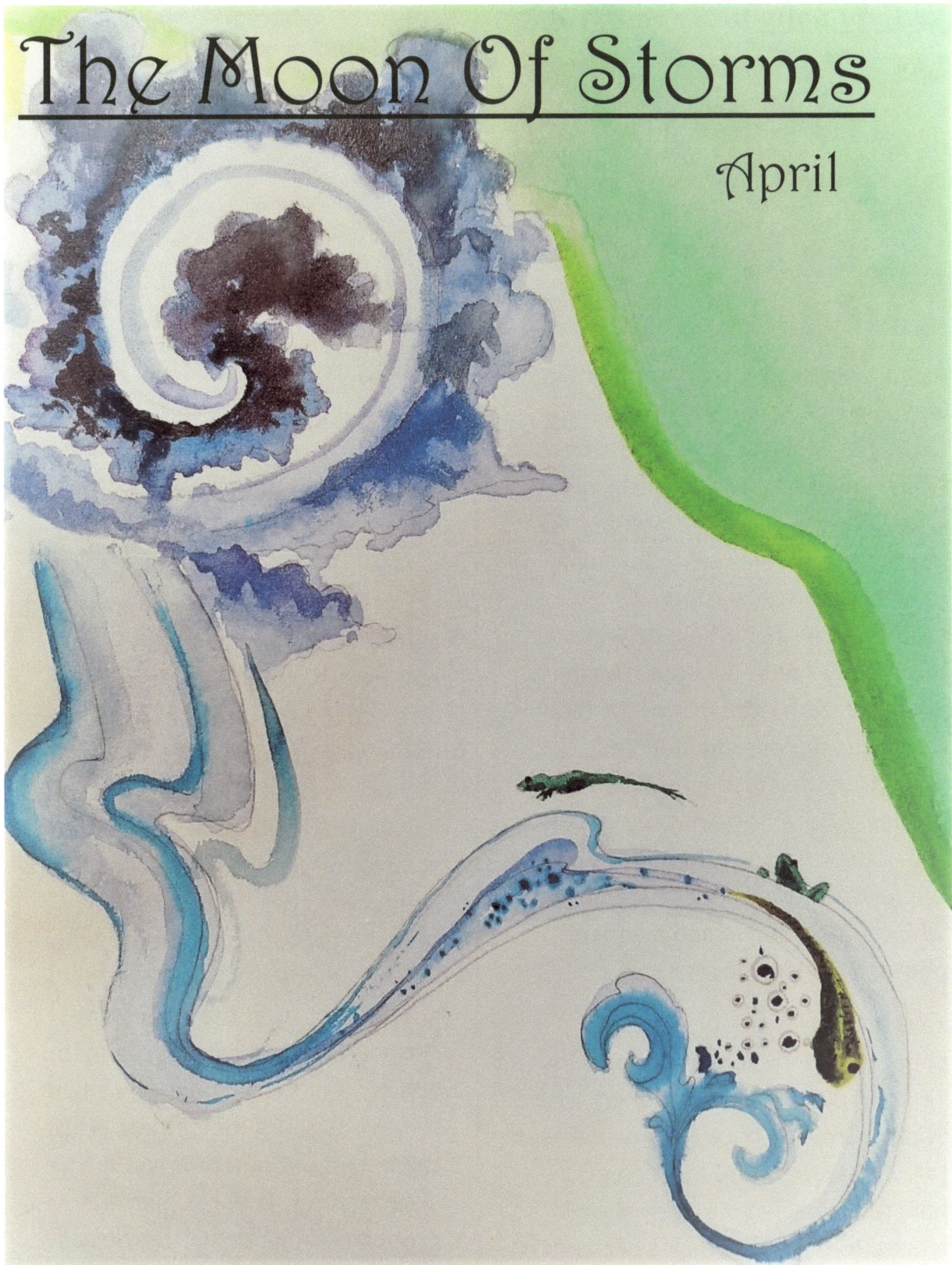

The Moon Of Storms

April

Yaupon holly (*Ilex vomitoria*)

As an evergreen plant, yaupon holly leaves are available year-round. However, the leaves are at the best when they are new and fresh, which is usually in the Spring. Yaupon may also sprout new leaves following a rain shower with warmer temperatures regardless of season though. By Autumn, yaupon bushes will try to concentrate most of their resources on reproduction and producing their distinctive red berries. After this point they usually will not sprout any new growth until the following February or March, when temperatures and average photo period increases again.

Yaupon holly is one of the most common woody species in Eastern Texas and the Southern United States. Growing between 4 and 9 feet tall, it has smooth to mottled gray bark and small, ovoid evergreen leaves. In the Fall, females of the specie produce small, singular bright red berries.

Branches and leaves of yaupon have an erratic and dense growing habit, in many places producing impassible thickets, choking out many other species. The invasive, toxic Chinese privet has a similar appearance, and can be found in much of the same habitat as yaupon holly. However, distinction between the two can be made due to the much more orderly growth habit of Chinese privet. Its leaves grow in regular, opposite arrangements down its straight, long stems, whereas the leaves and branches of yaupon holly are whorled and much more chaotic. Another key difference is that the leaves of Yaupon holly are lightly scalloped, which means they have very slight serrations along their edges, while the leaves of Chinese privet are always smooth. Also, Chinese privet produces similar, small berries as yaupon, however they are dark blue rather than bright red.

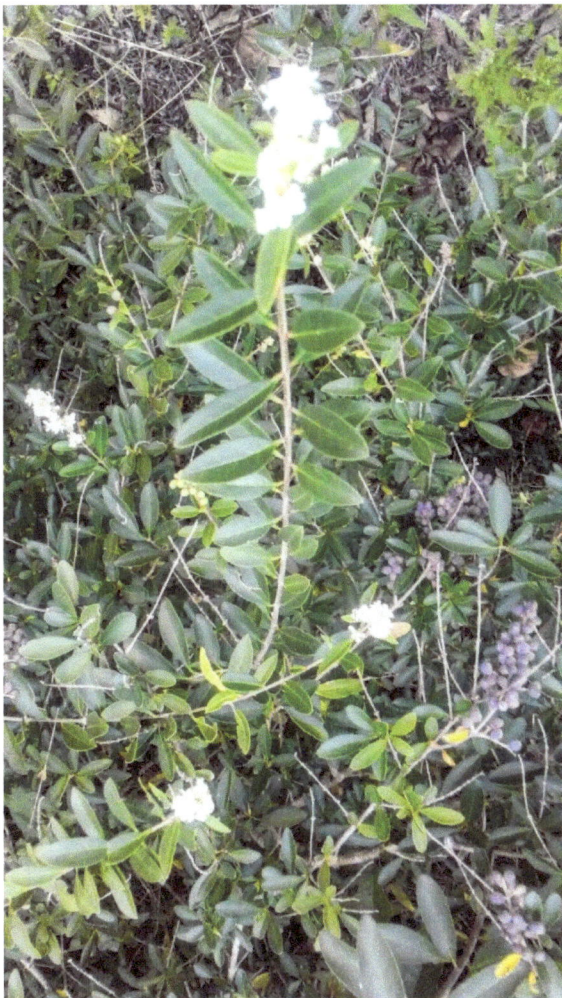

Toxic Chinese Privet

Yaupon holly loves to grow in damp, humid areas where soils remain damp or where standing water might be common. Originally, yaupon was confined to habitats along coastal areas, but with the suppression of fire over the past two centuries, it has spread to damp and swampy areas throughout much of the American South.

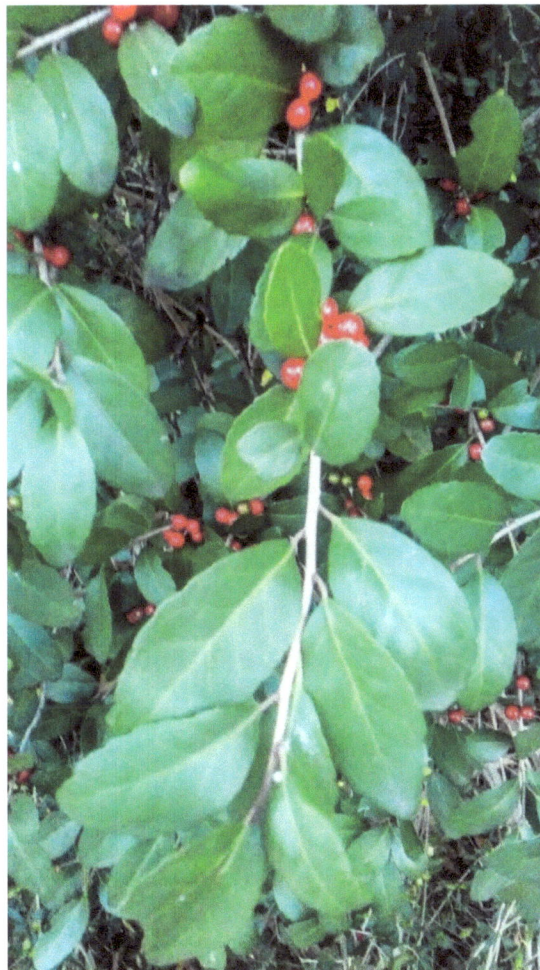

Yaupon Holly

Yaupon holly leaves are high in caffeine and collection is a simple matter of plucking or striping the leaves straight off the stems. Leaves need to be dried for 1 – 2 weeks prior to use or roasted like coffee beans. The drying or roasting process helps to break down the plant cell walls, to allow the caffeine to be better accessed. Afterwards, simply brewing as any loose-leaf tea yields a wonderful, caffeinated beverage that is enjoyed either hot or cold.

Yaupon, despite its invasive status, is an important source of food for migratory songbirds in the Fall. Pollinator species also visit the flowers when they bloom in the Summer. Although yaupon has become popular in landscaping, care should be taken when planting it due to its fast and adventitious growth habits and the difficulty of removing it once it becomes out of control. Where possible, planting should be done either in large, freestanding pots or in large, above-ground cement or stone planters.

Transplanting or propagation of yaupon is easily accomplished in late Winter or early Spring, before new growth has appeared. Uncovering and separating young, new roots from the parent root stock along with a portion of their parent soil and simply re-planting in the desired location is an adequately effective means of propagating this species.

Sow Thistle (*Sonchus oleraceus*)

Sow thistle begins sprouting in early Spring but is never really noticed until it stands about 1-foot tall, usually in late March or early April. Most other thistle varieties bloom at this time as well. They can also be seen growing earlier in the Winter, if there is a cold snap, with precipitation, followed by several days of milder weather with sunshine. Treating the cold weather much as a refrigerator crisper, thistle

plants thrive in the cool, but sunny weather common in the early to mid-Spring.

As a thistle, sow thistle has a distinctive, spiky appearance due to the presence of soft spines along the margins of its leaves. Its flower buds are also characteristic of the thistle family, appearing as small, green buds and blooming in two distinct stages. Several of these buds will appear clustered together, emerging from branched stems at the top of mature plants. In its early stages, sow thistle forms a loose basal rosette, but quickly shoots up into the tall growing habit it is most recognized for. As it adopts its mature form, its spined leaves appear to wrap their bases around the central stalk as they sprout. Common groundsel is a toxic species which has a passing resemblance to sow thistle. However, the leaves are blunted, as opposed to coming to points as sow thistle does.

Groundsel leaves also do not appear to wrap their bases around the central stalk as sow thistle does either.

Sow thistle can be found in wide variety of places, but most often in sunny meadows along the edges of woodlands. It can also be seen growing along the margins of small creeks or streams. Abandoned lots or acreages are excellent places to search for sow thistle, as it is a common colonizer of open or disturbed soils. Sow thistle is well known to invade domestic garden beds, and this can be another place to look for them, as well as a wide variety of other wild edible species too.

Harvesting and using sow thistle requires little preparation. The young, immature leaves can be enjoyed raw, as additions to salad or as garnishes on other dishes. As the plant matures however, it may become necessary to cook the leaves, as they become more fibrous with age. The un-opened flower buds are another delicious vegetable. They are wonderful pickled in vinegar with spices and may be used in a wide variety of recipes.

Like so many other late Winter, early Spring greens, the flowers of sow thistle plants are an important source of nectar for pollinator species. The leaves as well are foraged by a wide variety of wildlife species, ranging from cottontail rabbits to white-tailed deer. Sow thistle is one of many species which habitually appears in cultivated garden beds, but as an annual poses little threat of taking over the beds it appears in. Its presence can actually be very beneficial to insect species which in turn pollinate domestic vegetable varieties later in the year as well. As it is an eager volunteer species, little effort should be required to see it appear in your home or garden. Young plants that appear in undesired locations can be easily potted and transplanted however.

__Bull Thistle__ (*Cirsium spp.*)

Bull thistle typically appears later in the Spring harvesting season than other herbaceous species. Once the chill of Winter is finally gone and the sun begins to warm the landscape, between March and April, bull thistle begins appearing on sunny hillsides and in open meadows. After the Spring rains, they begin sending up their large, tall flower stalks. The large buds which appear in May ripen and bloom in June, when the days are at their longest. After being pollinated, the flowers enter their second stage and go to seed, to be carried away on the wind.

Bull thistle is an incredibly spiny plant. Forming a dense basal rosette, bull thistle produces spines along the margins of its leaves similar in thickness and length to those found on cacti. As the plant matures, it sends up a 3 – 4-foot flower stalk which can bear several flower buds on terminal, branched stems. The flowers themselves are many rayed and can be either deep purple or light yellow in color. The succeeding seed head resembles that of the dandelion, or other thistle species; dozens of small to medium sized seeds attached to white, feather-light follicles, which are easily distributed by the Summer winds.

Bull thistle loves to grow in sunny or open fields and meadows, where the soils are well drained and possibly more sandy. Pastures, roadsides, and abandoned lots are all good places to search for this specie. Unlike many other, smaller thistles or other herbaceous species, bull thistle is not easily crowded out by the large grasses which fill these areas.

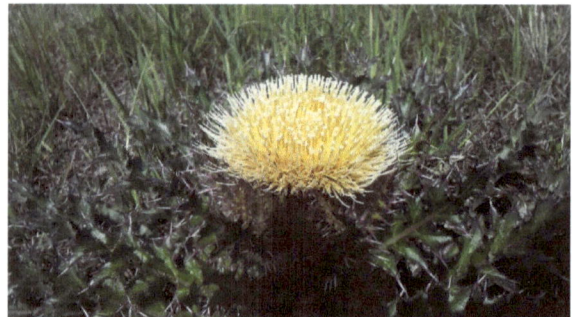

Great care should be taken to avoid the sharp spines when harvesting bull thistle leaves. The large, thick leaf ribs, as well as the central flower stalk can be boiled, or eaten raw, and used just as with celery. The flower stalk will need to be stripped of its thin, outer layer as it is rather fibrous and unpalatable. The unopened flower buds can be harvested as well and boiled and enjoyed similar to domestic artichokes. The out layers of the flower buds remain fibrous and spiny after boiling and will need to be removed as well, but the soft inner portion has a wonderful, floral taste which is worth the effort.

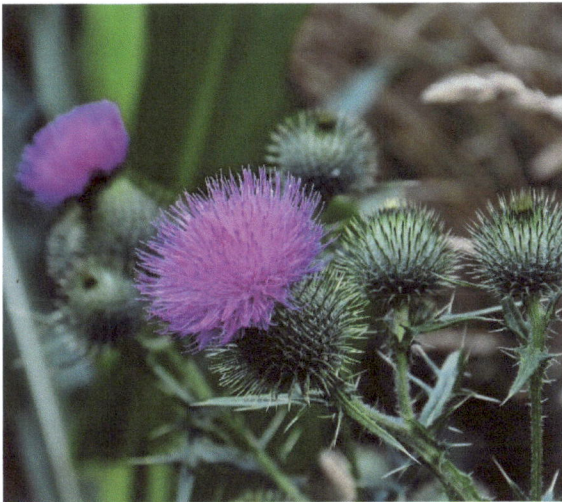

Thistle flowers are an important source of nectar for pollinator species, however most other species of wildlife avoid the plant due to its thorny spines. Should bull thistle plants be desired in your home or garden, they may be propagated by collecting seeds from mature flower heads in the wild and planting them in prepared pots or beds. Any plants sprouted in pots though will most likely need to be transferred to an outdoor bed, as the plant can reach several feet in height. As with all wild seeds, it is important to sow bull

thistle seeds after they are collected, as opposed to storing them until the following Spring. For wild seeds, it is important they experience the natural weathering processes of the seasons, especially in Winter, to ensure successful germination. Very young plants may also be transplanted from the wild to the garden, however great care should be taken to remove the entire tap root and as much of the fine root hairs as possible.

Corn Salad (*Valerianella spp.*)

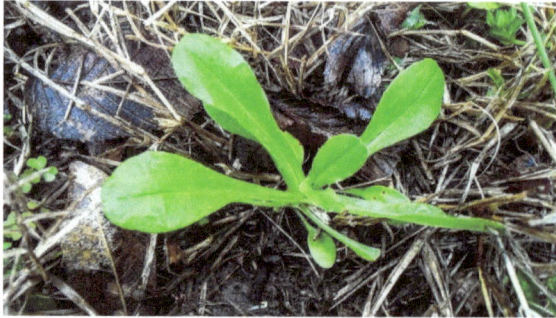

After the wild onion harvest in late March, corn salad begins appearing. Corn salad is an easy plant to miss out on though, due to its rapid growth rate. It grows quickly, and by mid to late April has begun flowering. The unassuming blooms are quickly followed by small, green seeds and then the whole plant begins to whither and disappear. The best time to harvest it is while it is still young, before the flower stalk and blooms have appeared. After this, as with many leafy greens, the foliage becomes more fibrous and less desirable.

Corn salad is an annual, herbaceous plant, with a small profile rarely reaching more than 18 inches in height. It begins as a loose rosette with a handful of short, club shaped leaves. The leaves sprout opposite each other and are alternately arranged at 90-degree angles. Once the slim flower stalk emerges however, leaves which are opposite

one another fuse into a single continuous blade across the plant's stem. The flower stalk is elegant and thin, typically branching once, about halfway up its length. Each branch terminates in a small cluster of tiny, 5 petaled white flowers. The seeds which quickly follow are also very small, round and are quickly dropped by the plant before it finishes its life cycle.

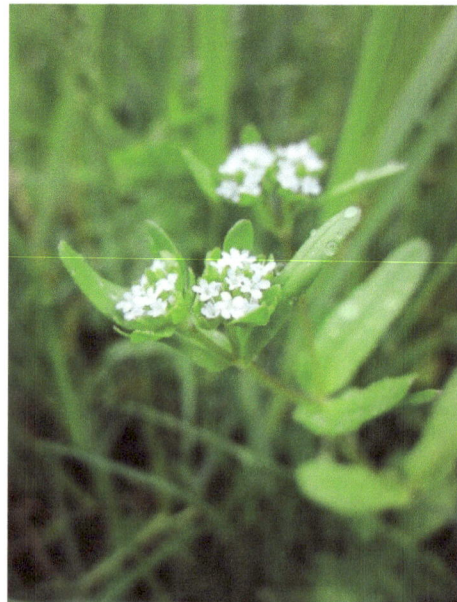

Corn salad is fond of open, sunny environments. However, it is easily crowded out by larger greens, or native grasses once they appear. It is an early colonizer of disturbed or abandoned areas, where it can often be seen growing in abundance. It can also be found near small creeks or streams. Due to the propensity for seasonal flooding, and the erosive forces which follow, these areas are usually stripped of their existing ground cover, and so are perfect places for corn salad to pop up. On rare occasions it may also be seen growing along the margins of woodlands. Due to the over-arching canopy and diminished sunlight, many larger and more domineering species might be suppressed, allowing corn salad to flourish. However, these conditions can be detrimental to the sun-loving corn salad as well, and so it is less common in such places.

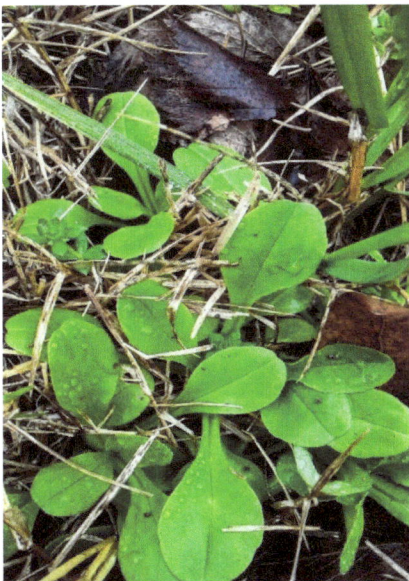

Corn salad, as with most Spring greens, may be easily harvested by the handful and stored in refrigerated bags until ready to enjoy. No special processing or cooking is necessary with corn salad plants, and it may be eaten fresh and raw. It is a wonderful addition to salads, and as a relatively mild green it can be used to dilute the flavor of stronger-tasting, bitter greens like dandelion or wild lettuce. Like other leafy vegetables, corn salad can also be eaten as a cooked vegetable, with minced garlic or onion, or as an addition to stir fries or soups.

Like all flowering plants, corn salad can have a positive impact on pollinator species. However, due to the diminutive size of its blooms, it is perhaps more beneficial as leafy forage. Many herbivorous wildlife species, as well as the larval forms of many pollinators, all enjoy this plant's nutritious greens. Due to its propensity to appear in disturbed areas, it can also have a helpful, albeit small, role in preventing further erosion from occurring. In planting for corn salad, due to its rapid life cycle and the small size of its seeds, the easiest method of propagation is to transplant several immature specimens to pots or prepared garden beds, before their flower stalks have emerged. This will ensure effective cross pollination and seed dispersal for years to come.

Mullein (*Verbascum thapsus*)

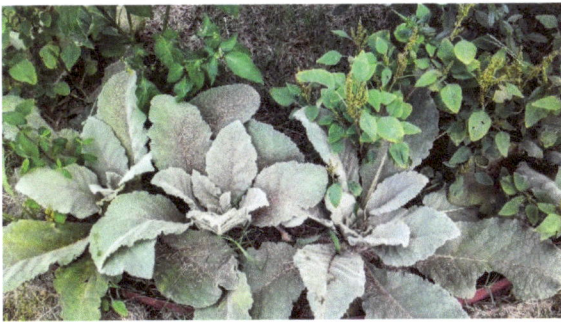

Mullein plants do not have an indeterminate growth pattern like many other herbaceous species, however they can begin growing very early in the year. For the first month or so though they are easily missed, but by the end of April they can form large basal rosettes, sometimes up to 2 feet across. Mullein has a two-year life cycle, and the first year it spends all its energy growing its leaves as wide and its tap root as deep as it can. In its second year however, it produces a tall, thick flower spike from the center of this large circle of leaves starting in May, followed by an eruption of beautiful flowers later that Summer. Soon after, the blooms are pollinated, and the stalk begins to whither. Yet the plant itself can persist well into the Fall and the dry flower stalk remain until the beginning of Winter.

Mullein, as mentioned, is a biennial, with a two-year life cycle. Its most outstanding characteristic are its broad leaves, covered in soft, fine, fuzzy hairs. The leaves are pale green, made to appear more so by the whiteness of the hairs covering them. The dense basal rosettes formed during their first year can be 1 – 2 feet across when fully mature. The flower stalks which emerge during the second year at the beginning of Summer are thick and tall, reaching up to 3 feet in height. These stalks are covered in densely packed flower buds which are also lightly covered in the same fine hairs apparent on the basal leaves. The flowers which begin erupting soon after are five petaled and bright yellow. They tend to bloom in waves, with those lower on the stalk typically opening first. The seeds which follow are very small, about the size of a grain of sand, and remain enclosed in the dried flower bud, to be shook loose by the wind or when the stalk finally falls.

Mullein is a sun loving plant specie. It is also very fond of well drained or sandy soils. It can even be seen growing in semi-arid conditions, so little is its water requirement. Large meadows in mature pine forests, or rocky hillsides in brushy uplands are all excellent places to look for this species, however it can be seen in about any relatively dry, sunny location. It is also fond of growing in disturbed soils and can be found in abandoned lots in urban areas, or in construction sites or pastures which have experienced recent tillage.

Mullein has been traditionally used as a medicinal plant, particularly with regard to throat or upper bronchial infections. Numerous studies have indicated it is effective at combating several different bacterial strains known to cause various pulmonary ailments. Harvesting mullein is much the same as with many other leafy, herbaceous species. The large, first year foliage is collected and can be used immediately, or dried and stored for future use. The most

effective means of utilizing mullein leaves is by infusing them into teas, with honey or other soothing herbs.

~Mullein flowers

Mullein flowers are particularly attractive to pollinators and their presence can help to attract them to the area. The plant itself is not unattractive, and its soft, luxuriant foliage can make a welcome addition to natural or water wise gardens.

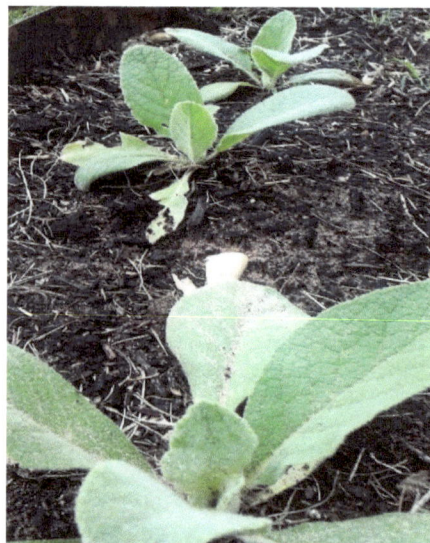

Due to its large taproot, mullein can also help to stabilize soils in areas which may be susceptible to erosion during times of heavy rains or run-off. A wonderful, and easy plant to propagate, young mullein plants can be transplanted from the wild, or any undesirable location, to large pots or garden beds. Any pot the plant is grown in will need to be relatively large, or else the specimen will need to be transplanted to a permanent bed before its second year of growth begins. Additionally, though the seeds are small, they can be also be collected and reliably sprouted as well.

"It is the Sun shining on the Rain,

And the Rain falling on the Sunshine"

-Frances Hodgson Burnett, The Secret Garden

The moon in May we call the Moon of Cicadas for the simple reason that it is when the high, shrill calls of the insects begin to fill the air. This occurrence is indicative of a greater change in the larger environment as well. The storms and floods of the previous month have started to ebb and in the heavy, buzzing humidity left behind, all manner of life have begun to hasten on to maturity. The days are full of the cries of a hundred different species of glittering insect, flitting from one blossoming flower to the next or else feasting on the luxuriant foliage rioting in the warm sunlight. The nights too are full of chorusing frogs and the trailing lights of dancing fireflies. As always, the storms of life are eventually followed by a calm. A time of peace, but also a time of buzzing activity and generation. Life seems so hopeful it almost sings with energy. A song so vivacious, the very land vibrates with it, to the tune of a thousand shrieking cicadas.

The Moon of Cicadas

May

Dewberry (*Rubus trivialis*)

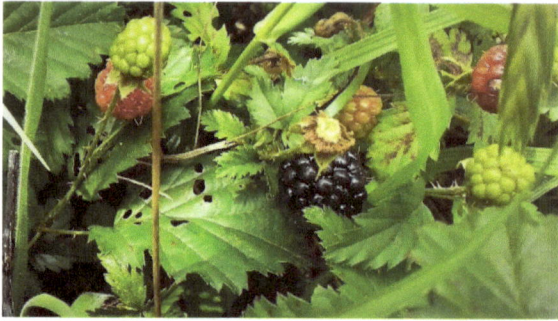

One of the most anticipated species, dewberries reliably come into season at the beginning of May each year. Their thin, trailing brambles and wonderfully fragrant blossoms are a welcome sight each Spring in late February and early March. By the end of April, as the Spring rains arrive, the fruits are just beginning to ripen, and a couple of weeks later, dewberry season is in full swing. In especially rainy years, not as many fruits may set following pollination, and once ripe they may quickly go sour. It is in the drier years that dewberries ripen in multitudes, forming veritable seas of fruit in good, undisturbed conditions. After the fruits disappear at the end of May, the vines spend the rest of the year soaking up sunlight and expanding their ever-growing network of thorny stems.

Dewberry, like its relatives blackberry and raspberry, is a thorny bramble with compound leaves having either 3, 5 or 7 leaflets which are highly serrated along their margins. Both the vines themselves, as well as the stems of both the leaves and flowers bear small, but sharp thorns. The flowers are simple and five petaled, with a delicate but beautiful scent. The succeeding fruits are classified as drupes, being composed of many individual seed-bearing fleshy bodies. The seeds are extremely tiny but are readily ingested and scattered by nearly every manner of wildlife species in the local area.

Dewberry loves to grow in sunny and partially sandy areas that do not retain water throughout the year. Abandoned fields or urban lots are good places to expect to see this species. An exceedingly tenacious species, dewberry will attempt to grow in most locations where its seeds are scattered to, and unless uprooted, will most likely succeed however. It is not easily crowded out by other, larger species and can even be found growing in sunny woodlands. Though tolerant of partial shade, access to sunlight is the factor which will limit its ability to truly flourish.

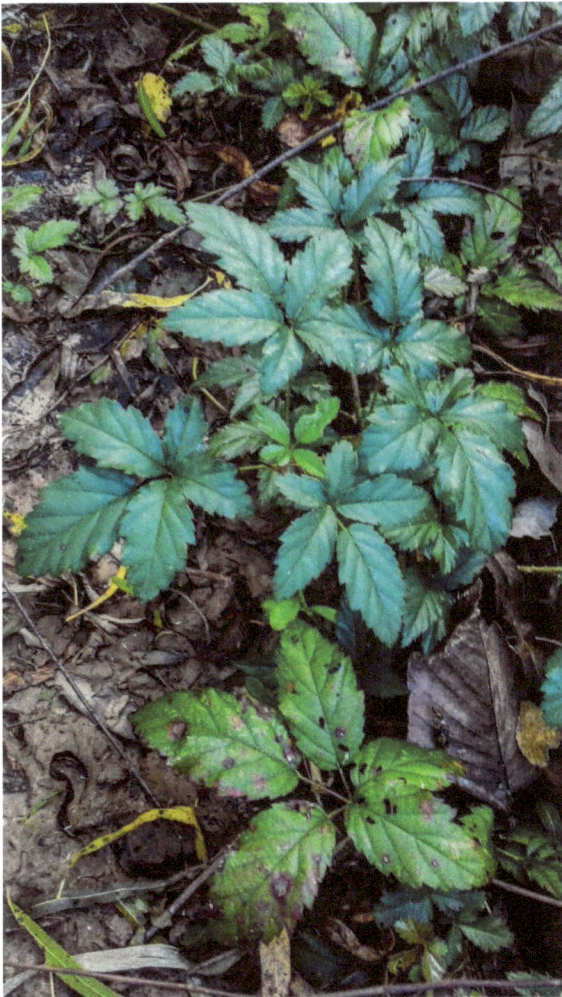

When harvesting dewberry, it is important to understand that without gloves or other protection, the sharp spines will most likely injure the hands. Due to the small size of the thorns, the scratches caused are rarely needing of any medical

treatment. However, a simple pair of gardening gloves is ample protection and they make the harvesting much easier and enjoyable. Dewberries are best harvested in groups, with friends, as the experience can take time (despite the fruit's abundance) and it is an opportunity to share in a rewarding pastime. Dewberries, like blackberries, made be made into any form of sweet treat or dessert imaginable. From jellies to tarts, the possibilities for this fruit are truly endless.

Dewberries, as can be imagined, are an important food source for a wide variety of wildlife. The flowers as well are an important source of nectar for pollinator species early in the Spring. Not many species browse the foliage or vines, except maybe as a last resort, and this can lead to them taking over many places where they grow. When planting dewberry, or any fruiting bramble, care should be taken to ensure the species remains in check. Dewberry is an adventitious species and is capable of reproducing from its rhizomes and covering wide areas. The roots and stems of dewberries are inedible and so the best way to manage them is to trim them back with shears or other tools. To propagate dewberry, the easiest and most effective method is to transplant root cuttings in late Winter before the plant has begun growing for the year. Should individual plants be found growing in undesirable locations, these may also be relocated to other areas as well.

Lemon Bee-balm (*Monarda citriodora*)

Lemon bee-balm, or horsemint, typically shows up after the Spring rains have ended at the beginning of May, when the humidity begins to soar. Like many wildflower species, the advent of Summer and increasing temperatures encourages lemon bee-balm to grow rapidly, its flower heads budding, blooming and going to seed in a matter of weeks. By the first days of Summer, at the end of June, lemon bee-balm will have begun to wither and scatter its seeds for the following year.

Lemon bee-balm is a member of the *Lamiaceae*, or mint, family. Typical of this family of plants, it possesses a square, hollow stem and bears complex, purple to white flowers along its tall, upright body. Reaching between 2 – 3 feet in height, it produces thin, lanceolate leaves with finely serrated margins, arranged at 90-degree angles along the stem. The seeds produced are tiny, being smaller than grains of sand. Several stems can sprout from the same root stock, and the species is capable of forming large colonies where it grows.

Typical of many wildflower species, lemon bee-balm prefers open, sunny habitats with well drained soils. A true prairie plant, it can grow with little to no water and is not easily crowded out by other tall, sun loving species (such as native grasses) either. It is a common sight along roadsides and across undisturbed fields and pastures and can be anticipated to return to these same places year after year.

The leaves and flowers of lemon bee-balm make a wonderful, aromatic tea. They may also be used as a flavoring or herb in a wide variety of other recipes as well. To collect them, simply harvest the mature leaves or uppermost flower heads from the stalks and either refrigerate or allow to dry for long term storage. By harvesting only the top-most flowers and mature leaves, the plant is allowed to still be pollinated and reproduce, ensuring a continued harvest for years to come.

Lemon bee-balm is a favorite of many different pollinator species, including bees and butterflies and even hummingbirds. The foliage and flowers are not readily foraged by many wildlife species or larval insects however. Yet, it can make a beautiful addition to gardens, and the benefit it provides to pollinator species can help ensure improved pollination of other species as well. To propagate the species, young plants may be carefully transplanted before any flower heads have appeared along its stems. Great care should be taken not to damage the thin, delicate stalks or the fine root hairs during this process. A simpler method is to collect the mature, dried seed heads, and plant them in prepared beds outdoors.

Red Clover (*Trifolium pratense*)

Blooming after the Spring rains, towards the end of May, and typically around the same time as lemon bee-balm, red clover is a much easier plant to miss however. Remaining rather inconspicuous before the flower heads appear, once the blooms do arrive, the plant is quickly pollinated and goes to seed, withering en masse. More often, the plants are seen after their season has begun to pass, but since they return to the same spot year after year, the location can be marked, and the plants anticipated during their successive season.

Red clover, like all clover species, is a member of the legume family, *Fabaceae*. The plants will rarely grow over 24 inches tall, but as a perennial, red clovers will reliably bloom in the same spot, every year, where they often form dense populations. Typical of clovers, they bear compound leaves in groups of three, but with a distinct white, or light-colored chevron present on the upper side of each leaflet. The flower head is easily recognized as a standard clover-type bloom, consisting of a dense inflorescence of light pink to red flowers, between 1 and 4 inches tall at the ends of tall, thin stems.

Red clover, as with many species of late Spring wildflowers, loves to grow out in the full view of the sun. Though somewhat competitive, it is possible for it to be crowded out by other species however, so large meadows and forest boundaries with plenty of sun, rather than open prairie, are excellent places to look for this plant. It is also common along roadsides, and occasionally abandoned lots or pastures as well. Red clover loves to spread out, and so environments which can provide it with full sun are generally also the places where it may stretch itself out and grow comfortably too.

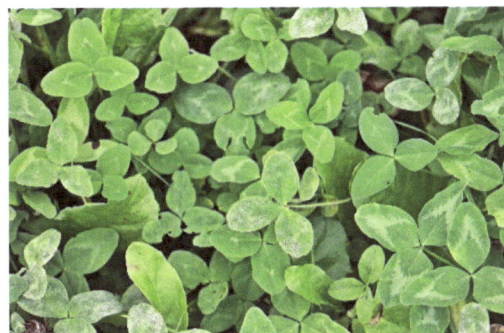

Red clover contains salicylic acid, the precursor of aspirin, as well as phytoestrogen compounds. Red clover flowers have traditionally been used as a medicinal tea for the relief of pain or to reduce the negative effects of menopause. When gathering red clover, it is important to harvest before the nutritious flower heads start to dry out on the stalks. Once they begin to do so, many of the beneficial compounds contained in them will have started to break down and disappear. This is why locating the plants early in their life cycle is so important. Once accomplished, handfuls of the flowers may be gathered in the same manner as any other wildflower. Care should be taken however, when plucking individual flower heads, not to uproot the plants. The root stock of red clovers tends to be rather shallow, and they can be easily dislodged if the plant is yanked too hard. After harvesting, the flowers can be allowed to dry and stored for future use.

Red clover, as a legume, actively fixes nitrogen in the soils where it grows. This has a beneficial impact on any species of plants which may succeed red clover in a given area, or which may grow alongside them. Red clover is also an important source of nectar for pollinators, especially bumblebee species. The plants are capable of forming dense colonies but are not overly invasive and are easily managed through the act of harvesting. When propagating red clover, the dried flower heads on mature plants may be collected and the tiny, round seeds collected from within. These seeds, or even the entire, dried flower head, may then be planted in large, prepared pots, or in beds with full sun.

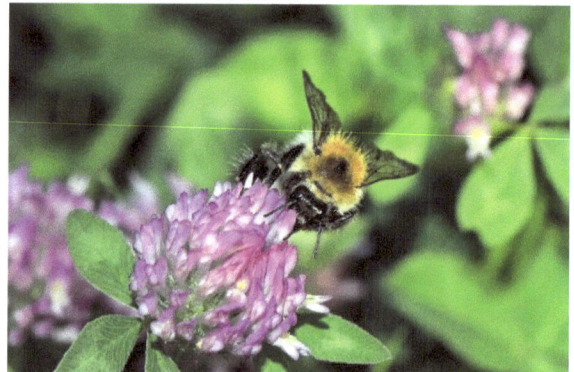

Heals All (*Prunella vulgaris*)

Another early Summer wildflower to bloom in May after the Spring rains have ended, and the air is thick and humid, is the small but wonderfully beneficial self-heal, or heals all. Similar to red clover, heals all can be a hard plant to spot before the flower heads have emerged. Like other wildflowers, heals all can grow rapidly, and is quickly pollinated and gone to seed before the end of June. The blooming of its flowers is rather staggered however, and the dried flower heads can persist on the plant well past Midsummer.

A perennial member of the *Lamiaceae*, or mint family, heals all averages about 12 inches tall, and has the characteristic hollow, square mint stem, with thin, lanceolate leaves seen in many related species. The leaves also have gently serrated margins and are highly vascularized. Leaves appear opposite each other and are arranged in alternating pairs, at 90-degree angles up the stem. The flower head is a club-like cluster, with a somewhat whorled pattern, growing up to 3 – 4 inches tall. The individual flowers are lavender to purple in color, tubular, with an upper and lower lip. The upper lip is a darker colored hood, while the lower is paler and divided into three lobes. The seeds are small, round, and remain contained inside the dried flower head once ripe. Heals all spreads both by seed and by adventitious rhizomes grown along stems which creep along the ground.

Heals all prefers to grow in sunny, undisturbed meadows and margins along the edges of woodlands. A common sight in fallow pastures, heals all grows best in moderately sandy soils which may have a higher moisture content, but which do not habitually retain water. Though it can be seen as a colonizer in abandoned lots or other areas, it is much fonder of undisturbed habitat, and so can be more difficult to find in urban areas. Due to its small size, it is very susceptible to damage from lawn maintenance, which can result in its flower heads being cut off before they can go to seed, thus prohibiting it becoming established in many areas.

Heals all is another wildflower species which is traditionally used for medicinal purposes. Its common name is due to its purported ability to cure a wide variety of ailments and was particularly used for treatment of external and internal inflammation or hemorrhage, especially of the throat and respiratory system. It is commonly imbided as a tea brewed from the flower heads or young leaves. It is also a common addition to garden salads, or even as a cooked herb in some dishes. When harvesting the plant, the flower heads should be carefully cut off, so as not to damage the rest of the plant. Young leaves may also be harvested, however after the emergence of the flowers, they may

become more fibrous and need cooking to be palatable.

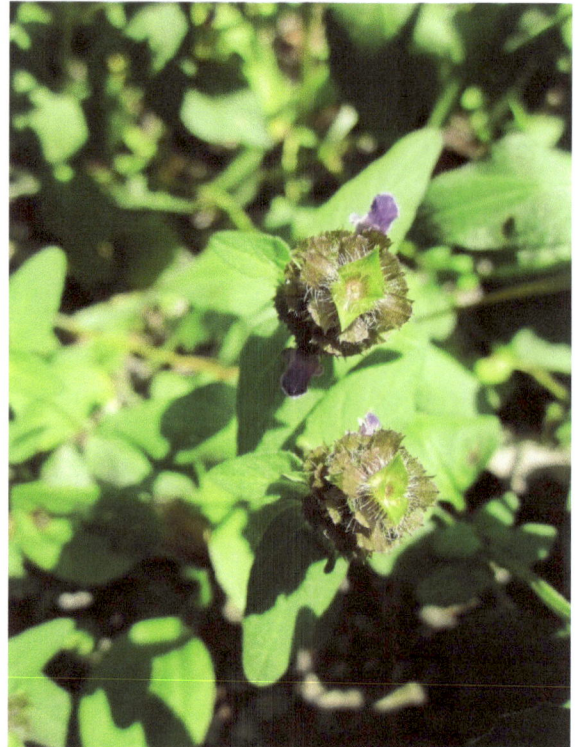

Though not as attractive as other members of the mint family, heals all is still an important flower for pollinator species, especially butterflies and native bees. Some larval insects may occasionally feed on the foliage, but it is generally avoided by most herbivorous wildlife species. To propagate heals all, young plants may be transplanted to pots early in the Spring. However, plants at this stage can be difficult to precisely identify in the wild, as they resemble many other mint species and are so small in stature. More effectively, ripened seeds from mature flower heads may be collected and planted instead. Heals all is an excellent container plant, and in garden beds, despite its adventitious nature, it is easily contained.

Purple Coneflower (*Echinacea purpurea*)

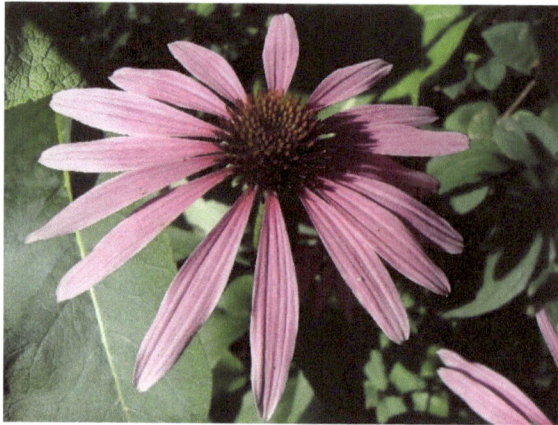

The season of the purple coneflower is a little longer than many other species of wildflower, often lasting until late Summer or early Fall if conditions allow. The plant begins growing during the rainy season, through April and May, and once the rains cease, it begins to show the large, characteristic flowers for which it is well known. These flowers may continue to bloom from May, through June and into July or August, and once pollinated, the drying seed heads remain on the stalk for many weeks longer. After the seeds have ripened however, the plant will begin retracting energy and nutrients back into its root, to store for the following year.

Purple coneflower is a perennial wildflower in the *Asteraceae*, or sunflower family. It sprouts every year from thick, woody rootstock and produces a tall, hairy stalk about 1 inch thick. The leaves are long and broad, averaging about 6 inches long and 3 – 4 inches wide, coming to points, and arranged alternatingly up the plant's stem. The leaf margins can be either smooth or serrated, with 3 prominent veins running down their length. Mature plants can grow up 3 – 4 feet tall in good conditions. The flower heads themselves are typically 2 – 4 inches across and consist of several ray florets surrounding a central disk. This disk consists of dozens of smaller florets, and has a distinct spiked appearance, which hardens following pollination. The seeds remain attached to the dried flower head for many weeks after ripening, before being finally scattering by early September and the end of Summer.

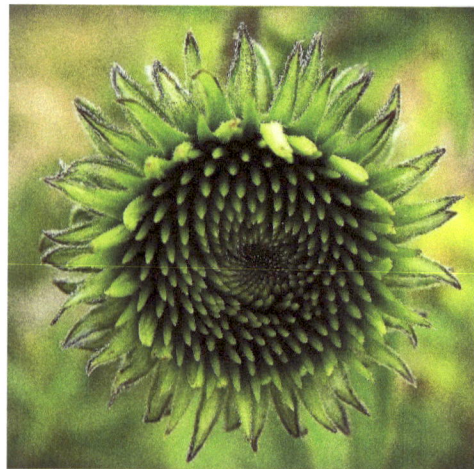

Purple coneflower is a true prairie specie and needs full sun and well drained soils in which to thrive. The large roots it produces grow best in sandier soils, wherein they can spread unimpeded. Due to its tall stature, robust rootstock and thick leaves, purple coneflower is a very competitive specie and is not easily crowded out by other herbaceous plants or aggressive grasses. It may occasionally be seen growing in abandoned lots or waste areas, but more commonly it is seen in undisturbed, mature prairie environments, or planted as an ornamental in domestic gardens.

Purple coneflower is perhaps one of the most well documented traditional medicinal plants of eastern North America, having long been used as stimulant for the immune system and proscribed for a variety of ailments. Though the leaves and flower heads have been dried and utilized in herbal teas, the rootstock is held to contain the greatest concentration of immuno-stimulant polysaccharide compounds. However, great care should be taken when harvesting the roots to only take a much as is needed, and not to permanently damage the remaining plant. Some species in the *Echinacea* genus are threatened in their local environments, and so care should be taken to protect, and propagate when possible these species, so as to ensure their continuation for future generations.

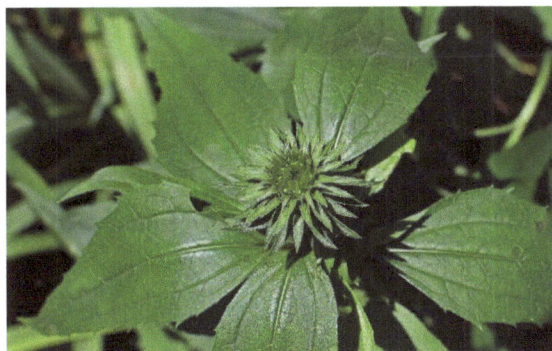

Purple coneflower is an important source of nectar for many insect pollinator species. Many species of migratory songbird are also fond of foraging the ripe seeds during the Fall. Purple coneflower can become overly domineering in planted beds. However, regular harvesting of garden specimens can help to keep them in check. When propagating this species, several different methods are available. The ripe seeds may be collected from the dried, mature flower heads and planted in prepared beds, or in container pots and transplanted out later. Young, immature specimens may also be transplanted from the wild to the garden. The large rootstock of these plants makes them ideal candidates for this method. However, all transplanting should be done before temperatures get above 75 – 80 degrees, as the higher temperatures, coupled with the act of transplanting can severely shock the plant. Root cuttings can also be taken from mature specimens in late Winter and sprouted in either pots or garden beds during the Spring too.

Cattails (*Typha latifolia*)

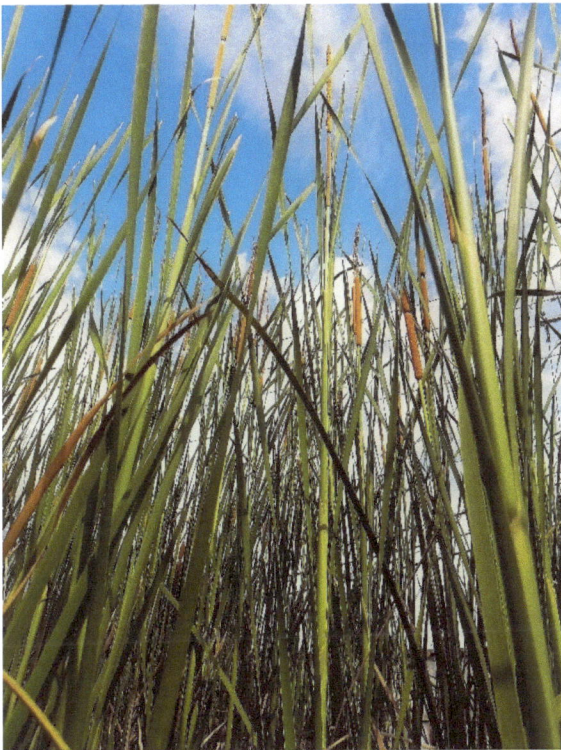

Cattail has been dubbed the "Super Market" of the wild due to its abundance of different resources and that there is always a useful part of the plant available throughout every season of the year. The roots are edible and may be harvested during the Winter months, although they can be very fibrous, with the edible starches needing to be removed. The young shoots which emerge from February through April, just as temperatures begin to rise but before the Spring rains have begun, can also be plucked and gathered. Once the rains cease, towards the

end of May, the newly growing, immature flowers are the next useful portion of the plant to come into season. By the middle of June, these flowers will have matured however, and produced a golden, windblown pollen which can then be collected. After this, the flowers quickly go to seed, forming into the thick brown "cattails" for which the plant is known. The soft, downy fluff can be used as stuffing for pillows or quilts, or even as tinder for cooking fires. By September and the beginning of Autumn, these fluffy, mature seed heads will have begun to dissipate, and the plants have re-entered a state of dormancy in preparation for the coming Winter.

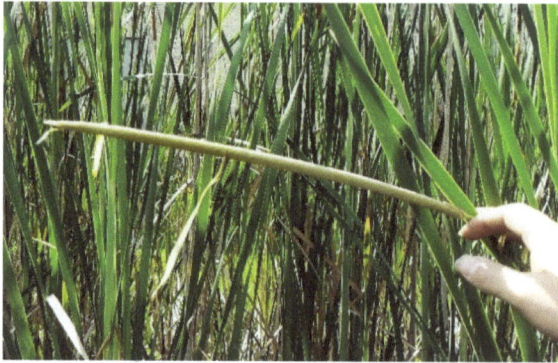

Edible Male Flower

Cattails are a specie of large, perennial, flowering wetland plant. They produce tall, thin simple leaves from a central base, which can grow to over 6 feet in height. Cattails have a tendency to form think stands and are a dominant specie where they grow. As such they are a hard specie not to notice. The plants' roots are a dense, interconnected network of white and yellow starchy rhizomes. The young shoots are bright green, turning white or cream towards the base. These very rapidly grow to be several feet tall, at which point they produce their central flower stalk. The flowers are primitive, growing as a long, densely packed inflorescence wrapped around the flower stem. Both male and female flowers are produced on the same stalk, with the male flower growing above the female. Before blooming, both flowers are covered in a thin, green sheath, and usually hidden in the midst of the plant's tall leaves. After

emerging, the male flower begins producing a fine, golden pollen which is blown by the wind to pollinate the female flowers. After pollination, the male flowers disintegrate, and the females begin forming the fluffy seeds, which are then also dispersed by the winds.

Cattails are strictly a wetland plant, and so they will only be found growing in or alongside slow-moving bodies of water. Swamps or marshlands are typical places to look for them, but also small woodland ponds or other relatively still water courses where they can get plenty of sunlight. As with many aquatic species, cattails have a real thirst for sunlight, and so shaded water ways are not ideal locations for them. Like all wild species, however, cattails are nothing if not tenacious, and have a tendency to spring up anywhere, provided the basic requirements of standing water and sunlight are met.

Each of the useful parts of the cattail are harvested differently, but none of them are particularly difficult to do so. Younger, less fibrous portions of the rootstock may be dug up and harvested in late Winter, just as new roots are being produced. These can be boiled and mashed, or even fried and served as an appetizer. Older portions of the roots will need to have the edible starches removed from the inedible strands of fiber within these roots. This can be accomplished by boiling the roots in sections, slicing them open, and then scraping the rich starches out with a spoon or other utensil. The young shoots which spring up in March are much easier to use. They may simply be plucked out of the ground by their bases, and then diced and cooked as any other vegetable in a wide variety of dishes. The male (uppermost) flowers which appear on the plants' central flower stalks in mid to late May, can next be harvested and boiled much like ears of corn. The boiled inflorescence can be eaten directly off the stem or removed and enjoyed as well. To collect the floury pollen, the engorged male flowers can be bent over, into either a plastic tube or brown paper bag, and shook vigorously. A single flower can produce a surprising amount of pollen, some of which will always escape to pollinate other plants, but a small container might still be filled within 30 – 45 minutes. As may be assumed, this pollen is a wonderful flour substitute or additive for many baking recipes. As a wetland plant, it is very important to be conscientious of any pollutants which could possibly be contaminating the waters these plants grow in. Cattails, like other wetland species, will accumulate any harmful chemicals which are present in the water, especially in their roots. Should there be concerns about the state of a waterway, any plants growing from it should not be harvested.

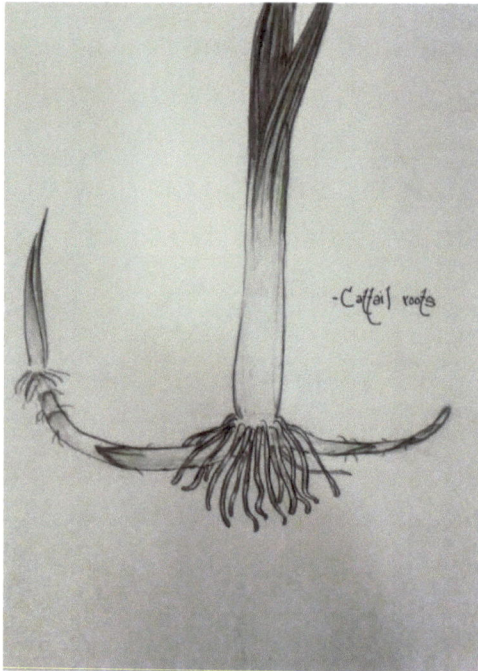

-Cattail roots

Cattails form a micro habitat within their environment. They provide all of the functions of wildlife habitat within one singular species. They provide shelter, as well as food and access to water, and a place to raise young and take shelter from predators. They are a favored habitat of a wide variety of waterfowl, and red-winged blackbirds have a particular fondness for nesting amongst them. They offer protection and shelter for immature fish fry, as well as countless amphibians and reptiles. Mammals, like otters, beavers, and muskrats also make their homes amongst them. No other species, except perhaps the great, sprawling oak tree, is capable of affording such a complete habitat on its own. In a word, what they really provide is a Home. Planting for cattails, however, can be problematic. Due to their tenacious, adventitious roots, they can take over an area rather quickly. If the design is not to plant them inside a contained area, or not allow them to spread over a larger area, regular control of their growth will be necessary. Fortunately, as with canna lily or other adventitious species, regular harvesting of cattails for food can effectively check their growth across a landscape. Should they be desired to be planted, transplantation of root stock, during late Winter before the young shoots have sprouted, is the most effective means of propagation. Later in the Spring, young, singular plants may also be carefully removed with as much of the fine root material as possible and relocated as well. However, by this point the roots will have stopped growing for the year, and so any damage inflicted may be permanent.

Greenbriar (*Smilax spp.*)

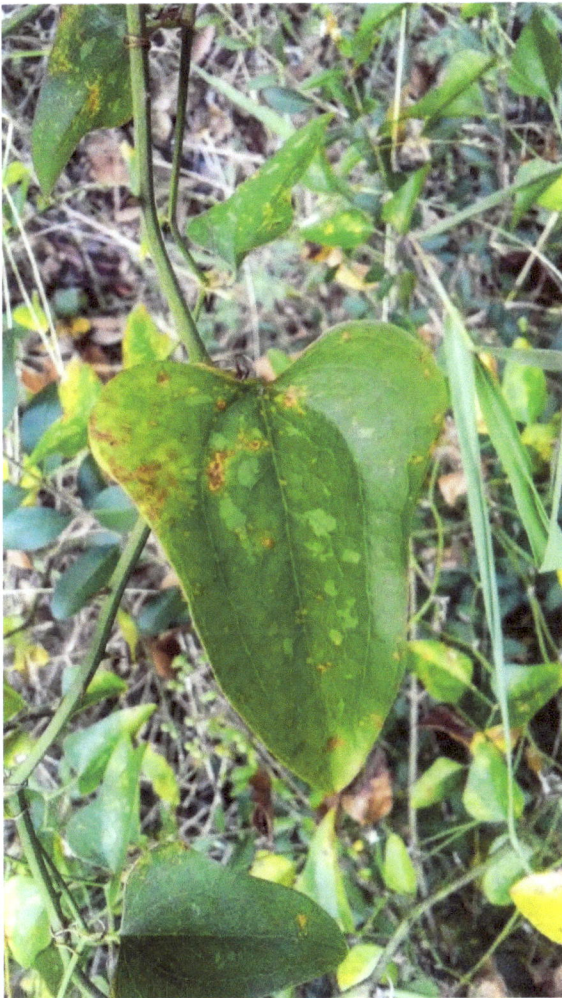

After the Spring rains at the end of May, and the humidity begins to soar, the thorny greenbrier vines begin stretching and growing their tendrils, creating razor-sharp labyrinths through the forest. Unless their succulent tips are removed, these vines will continue on weaving a tangled web until late Summer, when they finally begin to flower. The resulting, ripened fruits, which appear in the late Fall, are small pea-sized berries which reach near black in color and hang in loose clusters along the vines. Once the fruits have gone to seed, and the weather turns cold, the vines return to a state of dormancy, storing nutrients and energy in their large, tuberous roots. The trailing, barbed stems of their above ground portions remain year-round however, tangled throughout the trees.

Greenbriar is near ubiquitous across the landscape of Eastern North America, but it is best identified by two key characteristics. They are the only American vines to possess both thorns and tendrils along their lengths. Their leaves are also easily distinguished by their heart-like shape and their parallel, rather than palmate, venation. Bearing these characteristics in mind, on a brisk walk during the late Spring, hundreds of these vines may be spotted stretching their long emerald fingers up and out of the underbrush towards the sun.

Greenbriar vines are common across a wide variety of woodland and edge habitats. However, they are most likely to be found in dense forests where they have plenty of supports to cling to and climb up. Forested bottomlands are ideal habitats for these vines. They have a tendency to prefer more moist soils over drier ones, so yaupon thickets and small creeks are likely places to expect to see them.

The most sought-after portion of the greenbrier vine are the young, tender vine tips which emerge at the middle to the end of May. The vine tips are soft and pliable, and a gentle tug is all that suffices to remove them from the main vine. These portions can

range from 3 to 12 inches in length and can reach up to 1 inch thick. Dozens of these delicious, mild vegetables can be gathered in a short period of time and enjoyed in a wide variety of recipes. They are delicious raw, dipped in sauce and served as an appetizer and larger portions can be cooked, as with asparagus, and served with other vegetables.

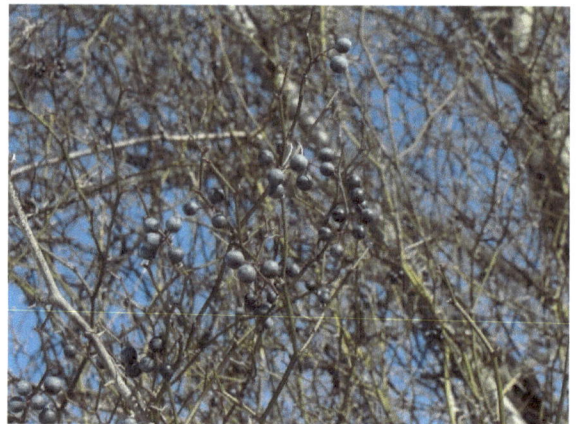

Ripe greenbrier berries[1]

Greenbriar is an important food source for a multitude of wildlife species. White-tailed deer will seek out and at times feed exclusively on young greenbrier vines. The edible seeds which ripen in the Fall are foraged by many species of songbird, either preparing for their seasonal migrations or storing up energy for Winter. Raccoons, opossums and squirrels also feed on these vines. Planting greenbrier vines can be problematic however. Because they have such a tendency to spread rapidly and overgrow a landscape, it is not recommended to plant these vines if they are not already present.

While an important food source, greenbrier can also form such dense mats of tangled, sharp-spined vegetation so as to make portions of woodlands totally impassable. Should the vines already be present however, with careful maintenance and regular harvesting of their new growth, they can become a valuable addition to the local habitat.

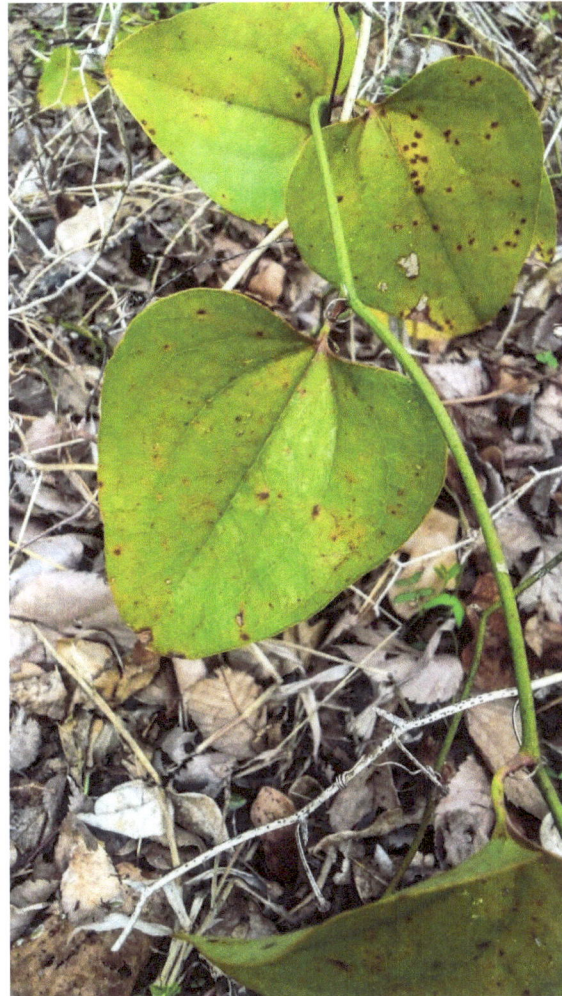

This month sees the returning of a great many species of fruit. The culmination of so much effort, for so many species, reaches its climax during this time. The days also reach their zenith during this month and the offspring of many wildlife species are now fully fledged or have opened their eyes and crawled out of the Earth, to stand and run on their own feet for the first time. Effort pays off in the end, and with the longest days of the year ahead, we begin to see the first fruits of all our labors.

The Moon of Fruit

June

Black Nightshade (*Solanum nigrum*)

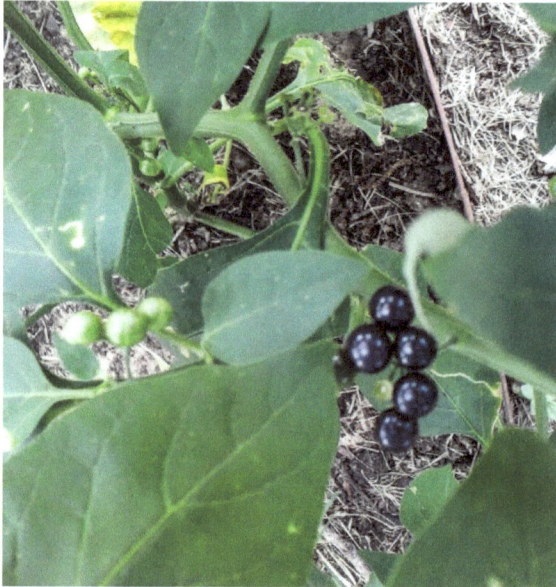

Another widespread species to appear after the seasonal rains, black nightshade begins growing in earnest by mid-May, and then begins flowering later in the same month, or in early June. The berries of this nightshade specie appear as a light green at first, and then ripen to completely black by the Summer solstice at the end of June. This specie will continue budding and flowering so long as conditions allow for it, finally withering around the month of September.

Of the many wild, native nightshades, few are edible, but the black nightshade is perhaps the most widespread of them all. As with most nightshades, its leaves come to sharp points, with prominent, palmate venation and the slightest wave or indentation along one side. The stalk of the plant remains green and may reach a height of 2 – 3 feet on average but can occasionally grow taller. The flowers are also indicative of the nightshade family; they are simple, star shaped and five petaled. Black nightshade flowers are rather small and white, with a yellow center.

Characteristic of the species, the petals of their flowers curl backwards towards their stems. The resultant fruits are pea sized, black when ripe, and arranged in loose bunches at the ends of branching stalks. The size, color and grouping of the ripe berries, as well as the shape, color and size of the flowers, are key to successful identification of this species.

Black nightshade is an understory specie, and so it prefers to grow in moist, open woodlands where it can still receive plenty of sunlight. It can also be found occasionally growing along the margins of forest habitat, or more rarely, in the midst of more open savannahs. However, without adequate moisture, it has a tendency to wither in the soaring Summer temperatures, or otherwise be prohibited or reduced in its growth. As such, sunny woodlands containing small creeks or year-round streams have a greater chance of hosting this species.

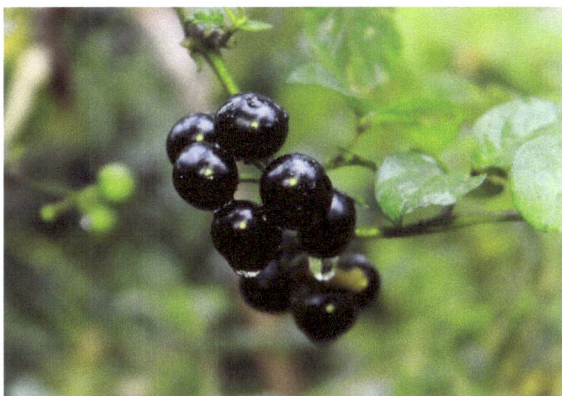

Black nightshade berries are as easily harvested as any other ripened fruit, and no special preparation or processing is necessary to render them edible or palatable. Care should only be taken to ensure that the

species has been correctly identified in the first instance, and that the fruits have ripened completely in the second. The berries may be used as many other species of fruit, in recipes for jams or jellies, or as a syrup or filling in pastries or other backed goods.

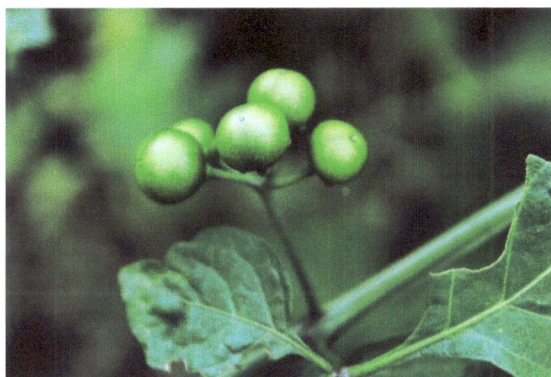

Black nightshade berries are a favorite of woodland songbirds, Northern mockingbirds in particular. Its foliage is also eaten by the larval forms of several different pollinator species. Black nightshade is an easy plant to propagate, and once established, has little chance of growing out of control, or of causing detriment to other garden species, or the local environment. Because of this, it is an excellent species to plant for. This can be accomplished by sowing the collected, overripe berries in container pots and then transplanting them out before they flower the following Spring. Black nightshade is also readily spread by the bird species which feed upon its ripe berries. A such, no planting may be necessary, as volunteer individuals readily appear in most garden beds with ample sunlight. These colonizing individuals can then be transplanted out to other locations, or put into large pots for future use.

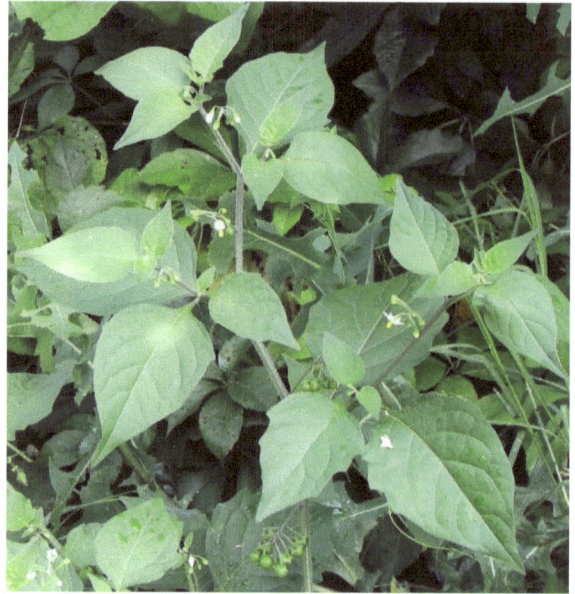

Solanum nigrum[2]

Mulberry (*Morus spp.*)

Mulberry trees begin producing their signature blackberry-shaped fruits during the Spring, usually in March or April. However, several weeks may elapse before the fruits are totally ripened, and they do not all ripen simultaneously. On average, by late May to early June, the first of the mulberries will have come into season. However, due to their staggered maturation rate, berries may continue to ripen for several weeks more. Mulberry season can last well through June, into July, if they are not all eaten first.

Mulberry is a medium-stature tree, with smooth, gray bark and deeply

veined leaves. The leaves are broad and deeply lobed at first but lose this appearance as they mature. The fruits themselves are drupes, similar to blackberries, and begin as a pale green, ripening through red to a deep purple or black. Thousands of these berries may be found on a single tree, during a single season. The smell of those berries which have dropped to the forest floor and begun to sour is another, potent indicator of the specie's presence, and that the berries have finally come into season. Mulberry is an understory tree which prefers partial shade to full sunlight. They are also fond of growing near streams, or in otherwise damp conditions. Damp, humid forests, with a well-organized understory, are excellent places to search for these trees. Those forests which might also contain seasonal creeks or streams are even better locations to look.

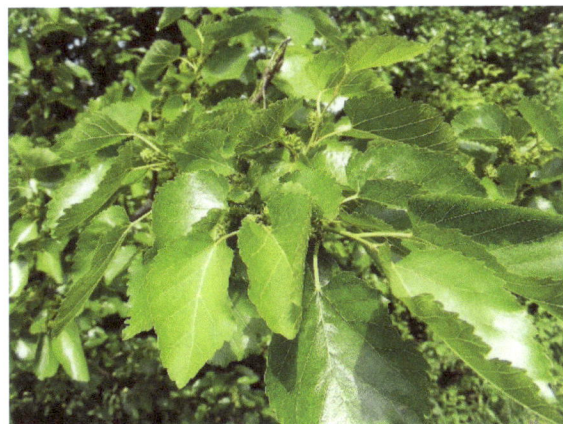

Harvesting mulberries can be more difficult than would first be imagined. While many of the berries which grow on low hanging branches may be easily gathered from the ground, they are also the first to drop off the tree or be devoured by passing wildlife. The majority of berries reside on branches much higher up in the tree, where they receive far more sunlight. Reaching these requires climbing into the crown of the tree, however mulberry trees can be difficult to climb. Making use of a short ladder to reach berries higher up is a much safer and efficient method.

As with many other carbohydrate-rich species of fruit, mulberries are foraged by nearly every species of wildlife where they are present. From songbirds to coyotes, all species can take advantage of the energy and nutrients that the mulberry fruits provide. As a fruiting tree, however, propagation is best achieved by

locating reputable nurseries with local or native cultivars. Unless the individual already possesses a wealth of knowledge and experience in the practice and propagation of wild trees from seed, root and soft wood cuttings, it is not advisable to attempt to propagate wild specimens, as it can be problematic at best, with little guarantee of success, and potentially damaging to the source tree.

Peppergrass (*Lepidium ruderale*)

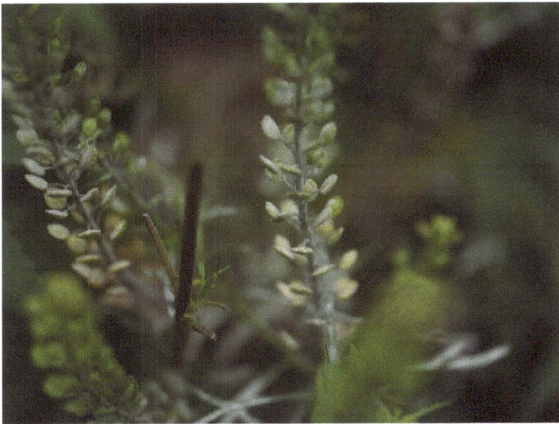

Peppergrass₃

Peppergrass begins growing in early to mid-Spring, usually in March or April, but it is hard to notice before its tell-tale seed heads appear in late May or June. After the Spring rains pass, the local habitat heats up and due to the abundant, ambient moisture it becomes extremely humid. As the sun's rays dry up what moisture remains however, the peppergrass seed heads begin to mature and eventually pop off, seeding the next generation. Having an indeterminate growth habit, several different blooms of peppergrass are possible to see in a single growing season, given the appropriate conditions though.

Peppergrass, or peppercress, is a small, herbaceous annual in the *Brassicaceae,* or mustard family. It typically grows to between 1 – 3 feet in height and can produce dozens of long seed heads on a single plant. The seed heads consist of a thin, central stem, with dozens of small, round seeds extending out from it. The leaves of the plant are thin and narrow and may become more toothed as they mature.

Peppergrass is an excellent colonizer species, similar to amaranth or corn salad. It is not uncommon to see it poking out of cracks in cement sidewalks or popping up in abandoned lots or construction sites. It is very fond of open, disturbed ground, where it can gain a foothold and access to sunlight before other, larger species begin to dominate the landscape. It is a common sight in urban areas, but it can also be seen along the margins of streams or creek, or other places where the forces of erosion may play an active role.

Peppergrass stem₄

Peppergrass seeds, as the name implies, impart a spicy, peppery flavor to dishes and are a wonderful and exciting herb for cooking with. To harvest them, the entire seed head is removed while still green and allowed to dry. They may be enjoyed while fresh but drying does help to concentrate the peppery flavor more. The leaves are edible as well, but by the time the seed heads have appeared, their flavor has become very strong and somewhat bitter.

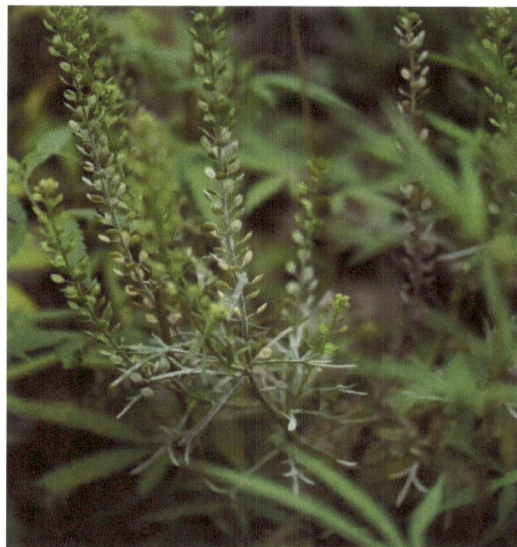

Mature Peppergrass₅

To propagate peppergrass, allow the harvested seeds to dry completely, then sow in container pots and let stand outside. As with all wild species, peppergrass seeds do best when exposed to the weathering forces of Nature, such as the rain and cold. These elements form part of a process that wild seeds need in order to germinate the following Spring. It may take until the following March to see any growth sprouting, but little maintenance or care is needed to see them flourish.

Amaranth (*Amaranthus spp.)*

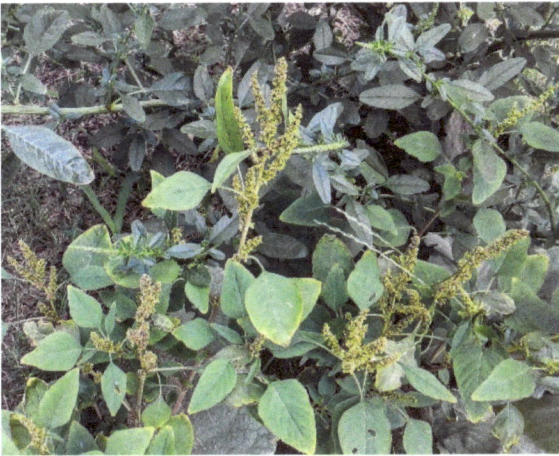

Amaranth plants begin popping up all over once hotter temperatures arrive and they days are full of sunshine. They quickly begin producing the signature seed heads which have gained them so much fame and enmity. Amaranth plants typically begin sprouting by the end of May, and by the end of June they can stand above 1 foot in height and have begun ripening their seeds. These seeds ripen quickly, just as the whole plant grows rapidly, and once ripe, the tiny seeds begin casting off in all directions with the slightest provocation. Several generations of amaranth will grow in a single Summer, and it has even lasted until late Fall and early Winter as well.

Amaranth is an herbaceous annual, with a tender central stalk and large, heart-shaped leaves. These leaves grow in an alternating whorled pattern up the plant stem, with those just below the seed heads forming a signature configuration of 5 blades in a star shape. Several seed heads can emanate from a single plant, either on the central stalk, or on axillary stems as well. These seed heads usually grow between 4 – 6 inches, but in some varieties they may reach over 12 inches tall. They consist of several thousand tiny, grain-sized seeds, which when ripe are easily scattered.

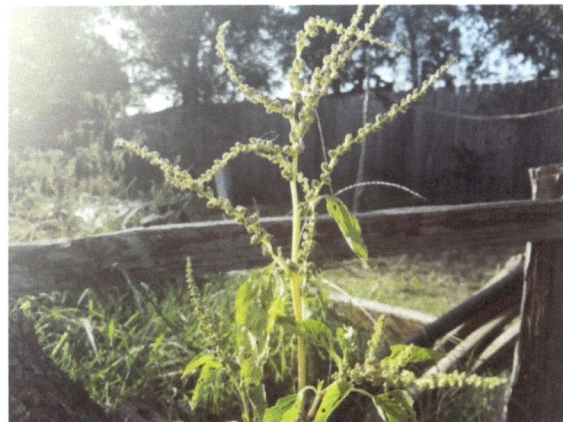

Amaranth, like many herbaceous species, is fond of open areas where it can receive plenty of sunlight, but also has access to ample moisture. It is commonly found growing along the margins of moist, bottomland forests or in sunny, damp meadows. It is possible for it to be crowded out by woody species or native grasses, so it is also habitually found in disturbed habitat, where it acts as a colonizer species.

Amaranth is one of the most nutritious species of vegetable available, and as it grows so prolifically, it is extremely easy to take advantage of. The large, broad leaves are a delicious leafy green, packed with beneficial vitamins and minerals. They can be enjoyed fresh, in salads, or as a cooked vegetable in a variety of dishes, similar to spinach greens. The ripened seeds can be collected and eaten just as with quinoa; either roasted or boiled with spices. To harvest them, carefully bend the seed heads into a brown paper bag or plastic container and shake vigorously. Some seeds will remain attached, if not totally ripe, while others will escape entirely, to ensure the propagation of another generation.

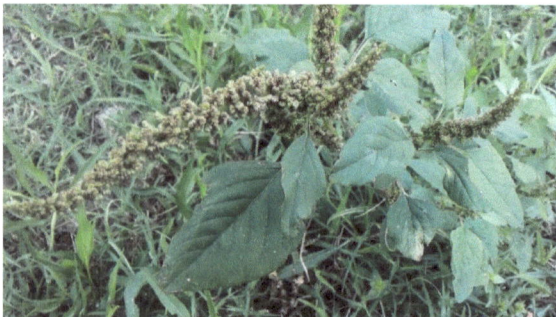

Amaranth is one of the most maligned, but also most beneficial species of plant in our world. Planting for it has the potential to do much good, both in improving the quality of

life for people as well as benefitting our natural environment.

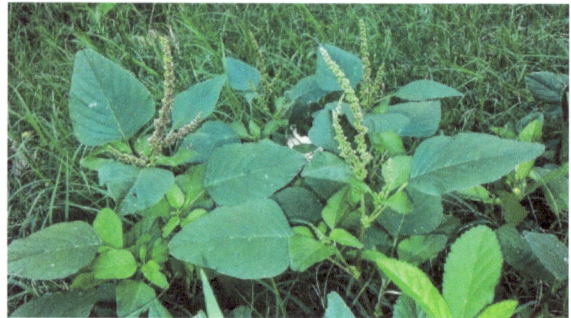

Amaranth leaves are a favorite of many species, from larval insects to large ungulates. Almost as soon as the young plants have sprouted, the tell-tale signs of insect feeding begin to appear.

The mature seeds as well, nutritious as they are, are enjoyed by many different species, but especially migratory songbirds and game birds. To propagate amaranth, the easiest and most efficient method is to scatter fully ripened seeds in large container pots or prepared garden beds. Depending on the time of year, these may begin growing almost immediately, forming the basis for several generations to come. Young plants that have not yet produced their immature flower heads may also be carefully transplanted, but should be relocated along with some of its parent soil in order to protect its tiny, delicate roots and avoid shock once relocated.

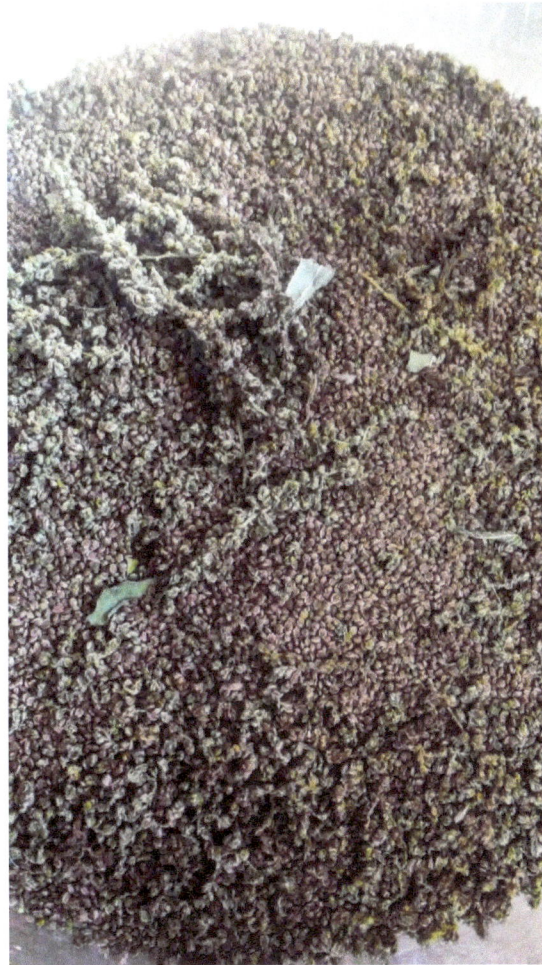

Wild Grape (*Vitis spp.*)

Wild Muscadine Grapes[6]

There are three species of wild grape in Eastern North America, all with their own season, but all three ripen during the Summer, when the sun is at its height and the days are longest. The first to ripen is the mustang grapevine, directly following the Summer solstice. Following this, the sweet muscadine grapes begin ripening from July through August, followed finally by the small frost grapes in September and October. As sought after as these juicy Summer fruits are, their seasons are rather long, as there are so many of them and their ripening can be so staggered, even across single vines. It is when they first appear though, in late June, that the beginning of Summer arrives, with the sweetest fruits of the year to hand.

All grapevines are woody vines with a penchant for being aggressive climbers, capable of covering trees, shrubs, and buildings alike.

Ripening Grapes[7]

At times, the trunks of these vines can reach up to a foot wide at their base, appearing more like small tree trunks, rather than creeping vines. On mature vines, the bark is rough and stringy, while younger branches are smoother, with many tendrils searching out purchase as they climb through the treetops. To identify between the three different species, the easiest method is to look at the leaves of each. Those of the mustang grape are perhaps the largest and thickest. Their tops are leathery and smooth, while their undersides are fuzzy and silver-colored. The leaves of this species can grow to over 6 inches wide but are often much smaller. Typical of grape leaves, they begin deeply lobed and then develop smoother margins as they age. Muscadine grapevine leaves typically have a smaller, more uniform size and shape, being decidedly more heart-shaped. They are also not deeply lobed, instead having prominent serrations around their margins. Frost grapevine leaves can grow to a similar size as mustang grapes, but they lack the silvery fuzz on their undersides, and are much thinner. Mustang grapes are the darkest when ripe, being almost black, and can be quite variable in size. Muscadine grapes are the largest, and typically a much redder shade of purple. Frost grapes are typically smaller than marbles, and a deep purple in color.

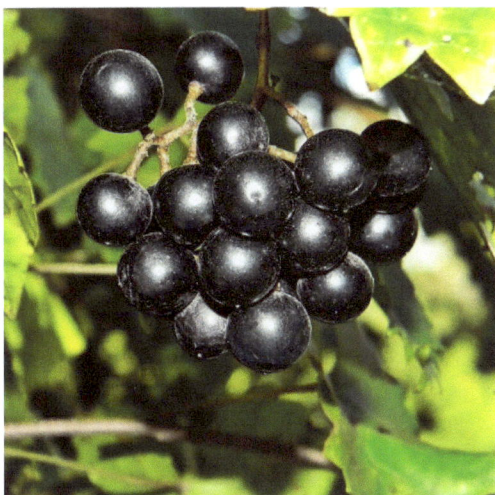

Ripe Muscadine Grapes[8]

All wild grapevines enjoy similar habitats; however, mustang grapevines tend to tolerate full sun more well than the other two species. All three species can be found in woodlands with moderately moist soils, although muscadine and frost grapevines do prefer more shaded and wet forests than do mustang grapevines.

Plucking wild grapes off their vines is nearly as easy as purchasing them from the local grocery store, and much more enjoyable. The uses for them are many, and perhaps only limited by the imagination. Mustang grapes, however, are quite acidic and can be unpalatable when eaten raw. All three make excellent jams or other desserts, and cooking with them in sauces or in beverages is just as enjoyable.

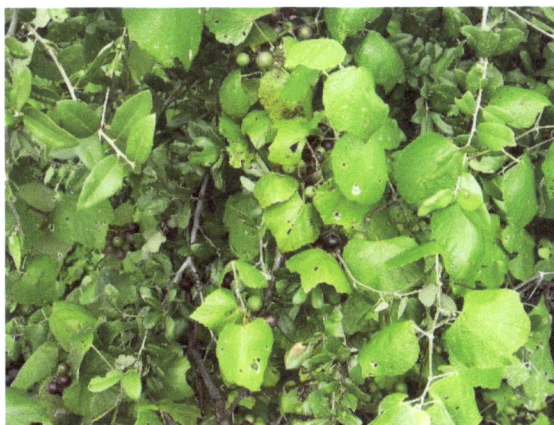

Mustang Grapes Vines[9]

Wild grape species are beneficial to many wildlife species. Their flowers are attractive to pollinators, and their fruits are a boon to all. Muscadine or frost grapevine are excellent vines to plant, if carefully trained upon a trellis or other structure. Mustang grapevines, however, can be very destructive, and have been known to cause damage to buildings and even trees, as well as generally dominating and covering the landscape. To propagate grapevines, the seeds from the center of the fruits can be collected and reliably sprouted in large pots or prepared beds. With all three species, regular care and maintenance during the Spring and Summer growing season is necessary to ensure the vines do not become a nuisance or begin to grow out of control. With dedication and patience, wild grape vines can be a delicious and beautiful addition to any environment or garden however.

Summer Solstice

"I almost wish we were butterflies, and liv'd but three Summer days.

Three such days with you I could fill with more delight

Than fifty common years could ever contain."

-John Keats, Bright Star

The young bucks have fully grown their antlers, and by the time they shed the velvet from their beams, some of the greatest harvests in the natural world will have begun. Though it may not seem like it, with the passing of the Summer solstice the days have already begun to shorten and the yearly life cycles of all living things, both plant and animal, have finally reached their zenith. All of the annual plant species have bore their offspring and having achieved that, begun to whither. For many species of insect, butterflies and the siren cicadas, their future generations are assured, and they also begin to pass into senescence. In the fullness of life, with a bittersweet sense of fulfilment comes a sense of impending loss, of endings.

The Buck Moon

July

Elder (*Sambuchus canadensis*)

In the buzzing, shimmering heat following the Summer solstice, the bright, fragrant blooms of the elder bush appear. Although the blooms are quickly pollinated, dozens of the large flower heads bloom at once, lasting until the middle of July. The small berries which follow are fully ripened by the beginning of August, but quickly disappear, as they are a favorite of nearly every specie of bird around.

Elder bushes are tall shrubs, or possibly small trees. Their limbs are slender and hollow, filled with a white pith, and are never more than a couple inches wide. Their bark is quite smooth and gray, with small, dark bumps or spots occasionally being present. Elder bushes rarely exceed 9 feet in height, with 5 – 6 feet being more common. Their leaves are compound, with each leaflet being slender, pinnate and finely toothed along its margins. The flower bracts which appear in the Summer are large, compound umbels composed of hundreds of small, white, 5-petaled flowers. These flowers possess a highly alluring fragrance and are usually buzzing with pollinators. The flower heads appear at the apex of the plant's individual branches and serve as a beacon which aides in identification of the plant. The ripe berries which appear afterwards are dark blue or almost black in color and about the size of small peas. Similar to the flowers, these berries are arranged in tight clusters, with each berry at the end of a single stem.

Elder is a semi-aquatic species, and as such it is especially fond of growing near water courses. It cannot endure the swift currents of larger, more flood prone rivers, but small, year-round creeks and other such water ways are ideal habitat for this plant. It does enjoy sunlight but is also found in partial shade at the edges of woodlands. Areas where small streams pass the boundaries of humid forests out into the open are perfect places to expect to find elder bushes.

Both the flowers and the ripe berries of the elder plant are edible and delicious. The flowers are traditionally made into cordials, syrups or another confectionary. The berries can be cooked into jams, made into syrups for cooking, or added to many baked goods or other desserts. Care should be taken, however, either during collection or at home, to remove as much of the fine stems attached to the flowers and fruit as possible. The vegetative parts of the elder plant are inedible

and have been known to cause illness or discomfort if ingested.

Elder is a key species, both for pollinators and as a general food source for wildlife. The flowers are an abundant supply of nectar, while the berries provide a source of carbohydrates and calories, as well as essential vitamins and nutrients. Elder does have very specific habitat requirements though, and planting for this species can be problematic if these conditions cannot be met. Without an abundant water source nearby, a large container pot can be substituted, provided the pot is large enough to hold a considerable amount of water, in addition to the large, growing root mass. As elder is a woody species, propagation from seed can be problematic, with no definite guarantee of success. A much more efficient method is to take root cuttings or young shoots from an existing stand of plants instead. Root cuttings should be transplanted in late Winter, before any new growth for the year has occurred, and young seedlings should be relocated before their first blooms have appeared and temperatures begin to rise.

Turk's Cap (*Malvaviscus arboreus)*

Turk's cap leaves and young stems begin growing in May, when the environment starts to become more humid and the days are filled with sunlight. By the middle of June, they are producing the beautiful blossoms for which they are admired, and in the warm sunshine these flowers fill with nectar and beckon to all forms of wildlife. As July comes to a close, and the humidity begins to dry, the ripened fruits of the Turk's cap plant finally come into season. Though they can be produced in multitudes, these rich, small fruits will not last long. Many different species are beginning to store up calories and nutrients, either for seasonal migrations or to endure the coming Winter ahead.

Turk's cap is a perennial member of the mallow family. It grows from several semi-woody, fibrous stems,

reaching on average between 4 – 5 feet in height, but with exceptional specimens occasionally growing upwards of 9 feet tall. The mature leaves are large and broad, with a roughly pentagonal shape and prominent, palmate venation. They are arranged alternately up the stalks, with the immature flower buds emerging where the leaves branch off from the main stem.

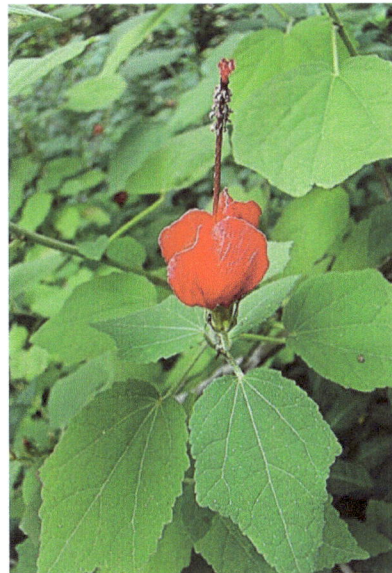

Turk's Cap Mallow[10]

The flowers themselves are perhaps the most recognizable characteristic of the species. They are bright red in color and never fully open, the petals forming a whorled tubule instead. The flower structure results in a cup shape which can hold a considerable amount of nectar. The fruits which follow are at first a pale green but ripen into a dark red and resemble

119

small apples in their shape. Each of them is roughly the size of an average marble, and is split into 5 different sections inside, each containing a small seed. The plant's roots are highly adventitious, and spread along the ground via fast growing rhizomes, as well as by seed dispersal.

Turk's cap mallow is a shade loving plant. Like many wild plant species, it can thrive in adverse conditions, but it does best in environments where it can receive at least partial shade, as well as a good deal of moisture. Turk's cap can be found in many of the same environments where elder bushes might be expected, however, the two are rarely seen growing in proximity in the wild. Turk's cap mallow prefers slightly more well drained soils than elder plants; its roots can suffer from too much

inundation and its growth be stunted or prohibited. Turk's cap is also a popular species in landscaping, and areas adjacent to these places are ideal for searching for escaped individuals which have returned to the wild.

Turk's cap leaves are an edible, mild green when harvested while they are still young, before their flower buds have appeared. They may be used as any other leafy green; as an addition to salads, or as a cooked vegetable in a variety of other dishes. Turk's cap flowers have perhaps the highest concentration of nectar of any bloom encountered in Eastern North America and are an amazing treat. The fresh flowers can be collected during the Summer, early in the morning when they are full of nectar, and used as a delicious, sweet topping for desserts, or made into jellies and syrups too. Care should be taken to not over-harvest them and totally denude plants of their blooms though. Without their blossoms, the delicious fruits will never appear, but more importantly, the reserves of nectar are a crucial food source for a variety of wildlife as well. The ripe fruits can also be candied, or made into jelly, or simply enjoyed fresh while lying in the warm sun.

Turk's cap mallow is one of the best plants for hummingbirds. Their flowers are an excellent source of rich nectar and are perfectly shaped to allow the small birds access to this resource. A wide variety of other pollinators as well, from butterflies to native bees, also are attracted to this species. The foliage is foraged for by several different species of herbivore, from cottontail rabbits to white-tailed deer, as well as the larval forms of many insect species. The fruits themselves are an important source of calories and nutrients, aiding species as they prepare for Autumn. Propagating Turk's cap mallow can be accomplished by separating young plants or seedlings before their blooms appear, or by taking root cuttings in Winter. The seeds as well can also be reliably sprouted, provided the outer flesh is removed. Because of Turk's cap's adventitious growth habit however, managing the plant can become quite difficult once established. Unlike canna lilies or cattails, Turk's cap roots cannot be managed through simple harvesting, as their roots are inedible. Cutting mature plants back in the Fall, or planting individuals inside large enclosures or in pots are both effective means of keeping their growth in check.

"Sweet, sweet burn of Sun and Summer wind,

And you my friend, my new fun thing,

You my Summer fling!"

-K. D. Lang

During this moon, the temperatures truly soar. The heat rolls through the thin, dry air and any clouds which happen by are quickly evaporated by the uncaring sun. Vultures circle high overhead while reptiles bask in the open. Though the heat may seem unbearable, relief eventually comes. The juice-filled fruit of the passion vine and the prickly pear help to slake the thirst of all, while the seasonal storms from the Southern sea quench the thirst of the land. In dry years however, the heat may continue, resulting in devastating wildfires, reducing whole forests to cinders. But whether hurricane winds or blazing flames, the result is that the debris and refuse of Spring are swept away, leaving the last great harvest of the year ahead.

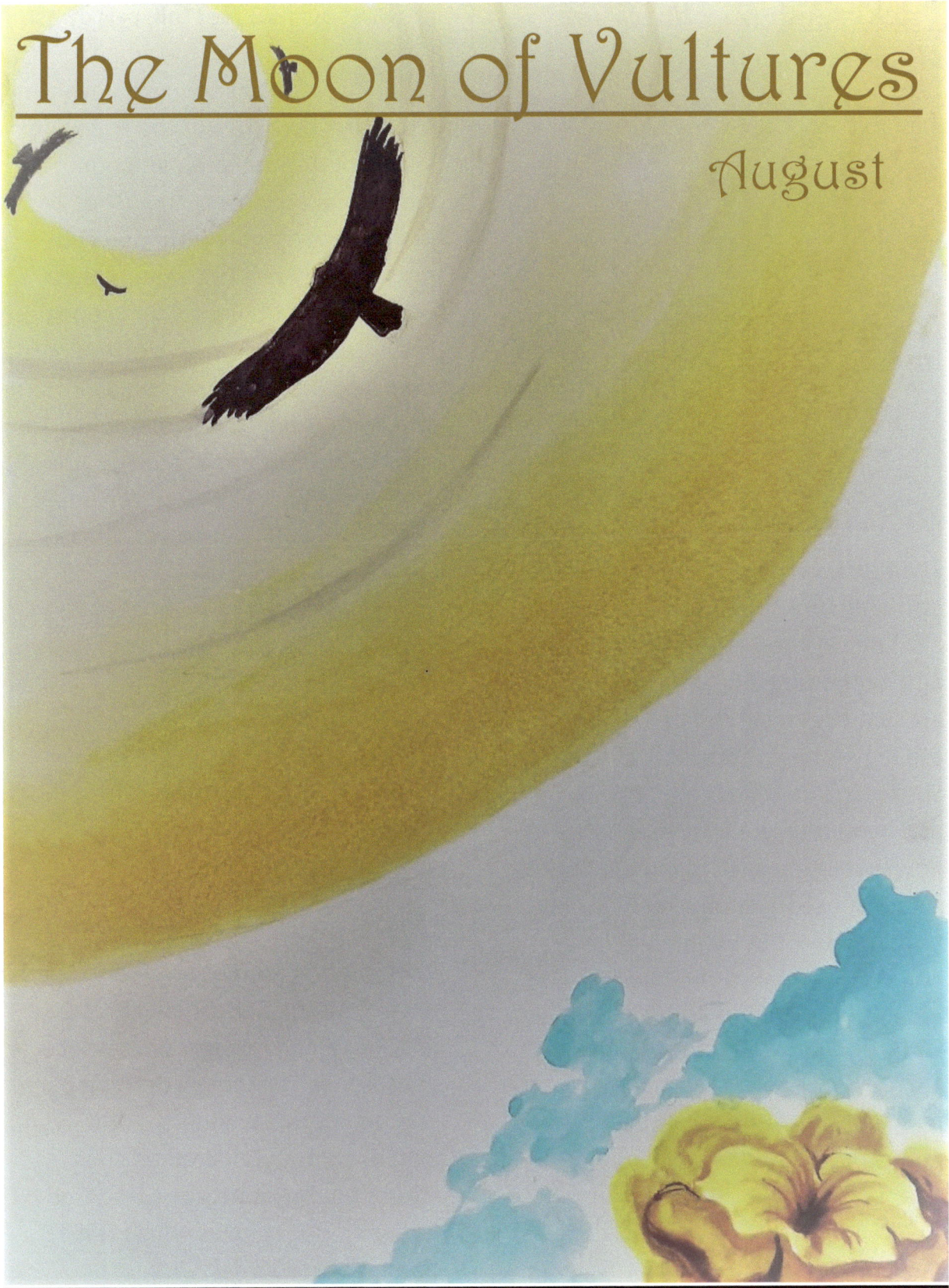

The Moon of Vultures

August

Prickly Ash (*Zanthoxylum clava-herculis*)

The berries of the prickly ash tree are one of the most unique resources available in the Eastern United States, and by the time August arrives, they are just beginning to ripen. Prickly ash leaves begin sprouting in early Spring, in late March or early April, and by mid to late May their loose flower clusters have bloomed. Their small, dense fruits take many weeks to fully ripen, but by the middle of August they have turned from a light green to dark red or maroon. Usually by this point the leaves have been devoured by insects, however not many insect species attempt to eat the seeds themselves.

Prickly ash is one of the easiest trees to identify in the landscape. Rarely growing over 20 feet tall, prickly ash is distinguishable by the small to medium sized spikes which cover the trunk and branches of the tree. The leaves of the tree are compound, with 7 leaflets on average. The leaflets are pinnately shaped with noticeable serrations around their margins. The flowers which appear in May form in clusters at the end of the branches. Each flower is small, round and light-green to white in color. The resultant seeds are about the size of a BB and a dark red to brown when ripe.

Prickly Ash Trunk[11]

Prickly ash is fond of more dry, open environments. It is usually found growing along hedgerows or fence lines, as well as the borders of sparse woodlands or savannahs. It thrives best in sunny, well drained soils where it will not be out-competed by larger woody species which can dominate resources.

Prickly ash berries are an excellent seasoning for many dishes. A related species in China is actually the main ingredient in Sichuan sauce. They possess an intriguing spiciness; the analgesic properties of the tree can slightly numb the tongue, even as the mouth starts feeling like its sweating. The same numbing properties are present in the leaves and bark of the tree as well and were traditionally used by peoples as a pain reliever for tooth aches or other oral maladies. When harvesting prickly ash seeds, care should be taken to avoid the sharp spines along the thin branches.

Prickly ash leaves are a favorite of many larval insect species, including giant swallowtail butterflies in

particular. The leaves are also occasionally browsed by white-tailed deer, and the seeds eaten by migratory bird species. Occasionally small specimens of this species may be found growing near mature individuals. Because it is a smaller woody specie, it is possible to transplant healthy seedlings provided extreme care is taken with the root mass. Fertilizer and soil amendments are always recommended when transplanting trees or other woody species, and adequate watering is important. Woody species should always be relocated before temperatures get too hot, as this can increase the likelihood of the plant suffering shock once moved.

Purslane (*Portulaca oleracea*)

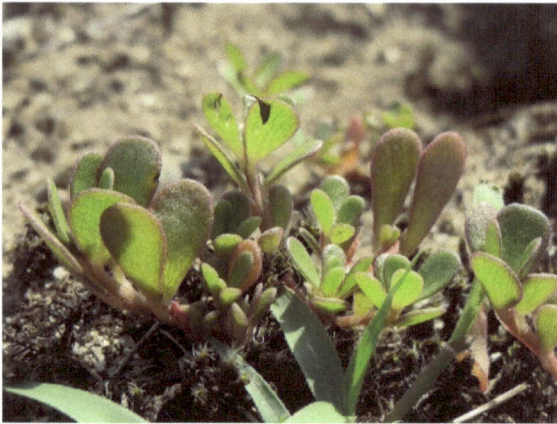

While all other species are wilting, or going to seed, the humble purslane begins to thrive. Starting in August, when the heat soars and the land thirsts for rain, when the ground cracks open and the vultures circle high above, the sprawling, homely purslane appears. By the end of the month, it will have flowered and begun to seed, but it will continue to spread and bloom until it is washed away in the Autumnal hurricanes or the weather finally turns chilly.

Purslane is an annual succulent in the family *Portulacaceae*, with a crawling, low growth pattern. Creeping along the ground, it produces thin, rubbery limbs and small, ovoid, fleshy leaves. The ropy stems are faint lime-green to pink or maroon in color, while the leaves are bright green. The flowers are also small, being not much wider than the largest leaves, with a simple structure and a deep yellow color. The seeds pods which form afterwards, are pointed and green, containing several tiny, black seeds. A similar looking, inedible species of plant, toxic spurge, appears at the same time of year. It is not a true succulent however, and its body and leaves remain thin and flat while purslane's grows juicy and thick. The sap of the spurge is also a white latex, while that of purslane is clear, if visible at all.

Purslane12

Purslane thrives in hot, well drained, but humid environments. Soils which experience a dramatic shift from Spring inundation to Summertime drying are common places to find purslane growing. Barren grounds and disturbed soils are also excellent places to search for purslane. It is a common sight in urban lawns and gardens, where it has long been considered an invasive weed.

Purslane Flower[13]

Considered a delicacy in many cultures, purslane stems and leaves make excellent vegetable dishes. Pieces of growing plants may be continuously harvested, while more are regrown throughout the Summer season. A wonderful addition to stir fries, as well as Summer salads, purslane has an amazing, delicate lemony flavor. As purslane is such a common herbaceous species, and is so readily propagated, there is little worry of damaging the plant's local population.

Purslane flowers can provide a source of nectar to pollinator species, and the seeds are occasionally eaten by several different species of migratory songbird.

However, due to the presence of oxalic acid, purslane is not as important a food source as other species common throughout the Eastern United States. Due to its low, sprawling growth habit, purslane can play an important role in securing soils in otherwise erosion-prone areas however, especially once these soils begin to dry out and become susceptible to unseasonable storms. Like all succulents, purslane is an exceptionally easy species to propagate. Thick, mature sections of stem can be cleanly cut from existing specimens and then planted in desired areas. These cuttings will take root of their own volition, forming young colonies of purslane in their new environment. It is important to water these cuttings considerably, as this combined with the high ambient temperatures will provide the humid climate necessary to promote successful root growth.

Passionvine (*Passiflora incarnata*)

As the hottest, most oppressive part of the Summer arrives, perhaps the most refreshing, juicy fruit of the year is just coming into season. Passionvine begins growing rather later than other species, usually not until the Spring rains have passed and the month of June draws to a close. By the Summer solstice, at the end of June, the first of their large showy blooms have appeared and 1 – 2 months later the large, juicy fruits have begun to ripen. Passionvine is unique however. Even after a single vine has begun to set its fruit, it will continue to produce new flower buds until the beginning of Autumn. This can allow for the appearance of both ripe fruit and new flowers on the same vine. Due to this, and the time necessary to ripen the large fruit, passionfruit season is very long.

Passionvine is a perennial family of vines which are very fast growing. As soon as they have sprouted, their tendrils quickly find purchase, pulling themselves upwards and over all manner of other understory species, and into the sunlight. The leaves are deeply lobed, coming to points with either 3, 5, or 7 fingers with smooth margins. The vines themselves remain green and non-woody, even in older specimens. The flowers are complex and perhaps the most iconic aspect of the specie.

They can possess between 7 - 10 lavender to purple petals, and a banded, filamentitious corona surrounding the anthers and stamens. The fruits which form after pollination are actually a large berry, commonly the size of a large chicken egg. The fruit begins a bright green, with a firm skin, but turns more yellow and wrinkly as it ripens. Very ripe fruits feel squishy instead of hard, and can emit a strong, fruity odor. Beginning in August, those that are easily removed from the vine are fully matured, with a dozen or more fleshy seeds contained inside. The seeds themselves are covered in a semi-clear yellow flesh and have a flavor reminiscent of bananas and tropical fruit.

Passionvine species are mostly native to tropical or sub-tropical areas in the Americas. *Passiflora incaranata*, however, can be found as far North as Pennsylvania in the United States. It prefers to grow in humid, but well drained forests with rich soils where it can still receive plenty of sunlight. Forests with rich, developed organic horizons along with permanent or seasonal streams nearby are places where these vines thrive best. However, areas which experience prolonged episodes of flooding or which are not as well drained, or which have a high incidence of erosion are not as conducive to the success of this specie.

Passionfruit are one of the most easily harvested species of the wild world, provided one has the patience to wait until they are fully ripened. Once they are in season however, dozens of these fruits can be gathered in an afternoon. Their applications are nearly limitless too. Passionfruit is a common flavoring in many commercial drinks and desserts, and the wild fruits are just as applicable. They are great added to any dessert recipe, whether baked or not, and are even more delicious raw, fresh off the vine. The ripe fruit can easily be added to any drink or dessert, and passionfruit margaritas, and other drinks, are an exciting, seasonal favorite which requires little effort or preparation. Passionvine leaves have also been traditionally used as a non-narcotic sedative and anti-insomniac.

Passionvine is an important species for a wide variety of insect species, but its foliage is an important food source to the larval Gulf fritillary butterfly in particular. The fruits, also, are a gift to nearly every species of wildlife present in the local environment. To propagate passionvine, the most efficient method is to gather the ripe seeds from mature fruits and sow them in prepared garden beds or large pots.

Similar to wild grape vines, passionvine can become a dominant species in a landscape, to the detriment of other species present, and so prepared structures for the

vines to grow along are well recommended. Young, emergent specimens may be collected and transplanted early in the Summer as well, provided ample watering is afforded. Temperatures during this time of year can be extremely high, and so transplanting any specimen during this time can be dangerous however.

- Passionvine

Mesquite (*Prosopis glandulosa*)

Towards the end of August, when the air buzzes with the heat, and whirs with the wings of insects, the fruit of the thorned, wispy mesquite tree come into season. The first of what may be termed the "Harvest season" crops of the wild, mesquite beans may be stored for many months. The flowers first appear in May or June, and by July are beginning to ripen. In dry years, the beans may remain on the trees until the beginning of Autumn, at the end of September.

Technically a legume in the *Fabaceae* family, mesquite trees are one of several desert-adapted trees to have made their way into the Eastern

United States during the past several centuries. Typically growing between 20 – 30 feet tall, it can reach heights of up to 50 feet in time, however it grows rather slowly. The leaves are pinnately formed, with many small, thin leaflets growing off one of two main stems forming each complete leaf. The bark of the mesquite tree is smooth, but finely textured, similar to sandpaper, and covered in sharp, 2-inch thorns. The mature beans ripen to a golden-yellow color but start out a lime green. Thousands of these beans may be present on a single tree during a good year.

Mesquite can be found in sandy, well-drained, sunny environments. As a desert adapted specie, and despite its prevalence, the humid weather of the Easter U.S. does not promote as healthy of fruits for the species as more arid regions do. A common sight in pastures and other grazed areas, mesquite was spread throughout the Eastern U.S. by early cattle herds traveling North from Western lands, and now it has become a nuisance in many places as a result.

The fruits of the tree tend to fare better during dry or drought-laden years, as more humid conditions can invite considerable insect damage followed by rampant fungal infections. It is a common practice to never gather beans which have already fallen from the tree to the ground, as well as those which may show the excavations of burrowing insect species.

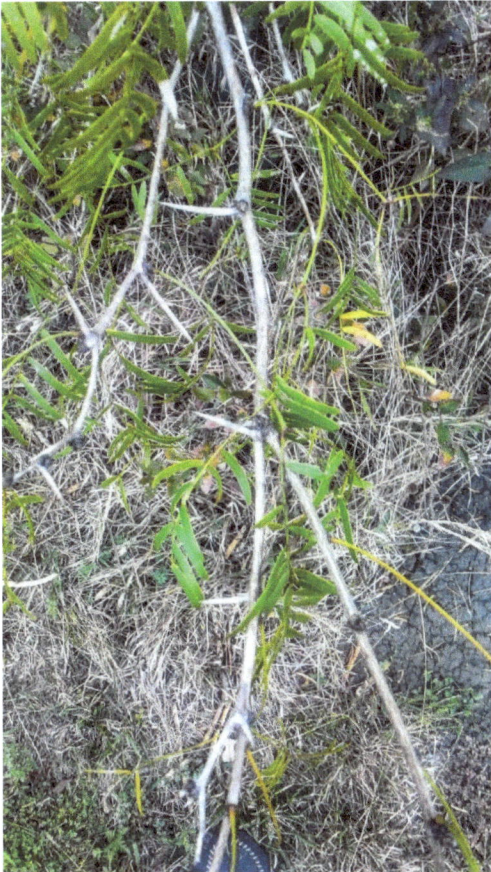

Such predations can lead to dangerous aflatoxin fungal infections. These cautions notwithstanding, several hundred beans may be gathered in an hour's time from a single, healthy tree during a late Summer afternoon. These beans can be stored for many months and used

as the basis for some of the most delicious wild dishes available. Mesquite flour is a wonderful food source, rich in protein and fructose. As such, it is acceptable for individuals suffering from diabetes or other heart-related issues. The chafe left behind from grinding the mature beans into flour may be boiled and the resultant juices used to produce a sweet flavored honey substitute or jelly as well.

Propagation of mesquite trees is not encouraged nor advisable. Mesquite taproots can be over 100-feet in length and are known to considerably lower the local water table, to the detriment of the surrounding environment. Mature trees can be exceedingly difficult and expensive to remove, and so caution is urged when disposing of unused chafe or seeds. By the same token, however, the consistent harvesting of beans

from existent trees can help to prohibit their propagation in the future.

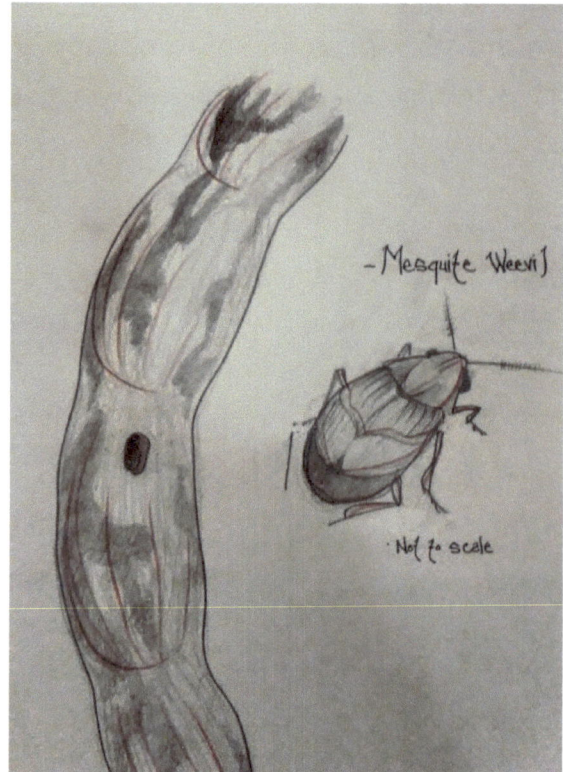

The greatest harvest of the year arrives during this month, providing a cornucopia of nutritious food and energy, capable of sustaining life through the Winter ahead and even into the Spring beyond. So much effort goes into the feast now being laid, yet in its ending, its return is also assured. By partaking of the seeds, fruits and nuts ripening during this time, we all contribute to their dispersal, and so ensure the efforts of the species who provided them during the past growing season were not in vain. Wildlife species too, whether short-lived insects at the end of their single year, or longer-lived mammals and birds, nearing the end of a life spent caring for future generations, feel not a sense of loss, but a profound sense of accomplishment, a lasting feeling of awe, and perhaps, the knowing of hope for what awaits.

The Harvest Moon

September

Peppervine (*Ampelopsis arborea*)

Loving the hot, rolling heat of late Summer, peppervine does not begin ripening its fruits until late August or early September. It begins growing for the year during the hot, humid conditions of late May and early June. By the Summer solstice at the end of June, the vines will have begun producing their small flower clusters too. Though their blooms may be quickly pollinated, peppervine berries may still take until the end of Summer, in September, to begin ripening.

A woody, perennial vine, similar to wild grape or passionvine, peppervines can grow quite prolifically and are capable of forming think curtains of vegetation. Hanging down from tree tops, or draped across smaller shrubs, peppervine produces compound leaves with deeply serrated leaflets and palmate venation. The flowers of the species are small, green to white in color, and simple with 5 petals. The flowers form in bunches, similar to the flowers of wild grape vines or prickly ash trees. The clusters of berries which ripen at the end of Summer resemble small frost grapes in appearance, beginning green to pink at first, but ripening to nearly black in color eventually. As soon as the mature fruits have gone to seed, the vine begins dropping its leaves in preparation for the coming cold season.

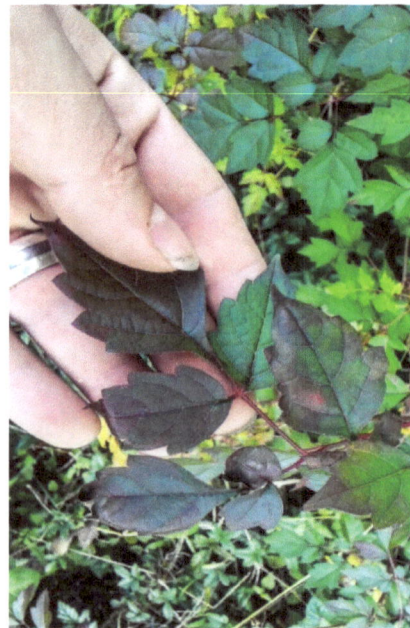

Peppervine grows in much the same humid forest habitat as many other fruiting vine species native to Eastern North America. It prefers moist, rich, but well drained soils where it can find plenty of sunlight. Peppervine is common to find in areas where wild grape vines grow, however, it is not usually seen growing in the same locations as passionvine. Whether this is coincidence or an interaction between species is unknown.

Ripening Peppervine[14]

Pepppervine fruits should be cooked before they are eaten. A form of calcium carbonate present in the raw fruits can cause discomfort or itching when ingested, hence the common name. Upon cooking or straining, this compound is denatured and discarded, leaving a sweet puree reminiscent of mild grape of blackberry flavors. They may be used as any other sweet fruits; in jellies or syrups, or any other of many dessert options.

Peppervine is an important species for migratory songbirds, as it provides a source of calories and nutrients in the preceding weeks before seasonal migrations take place. Hibernating mammalian species also occasionally forage on the vines in preparation for Winter. Planting peppervine, however, can involve a considerable amount of active management. The only useful portion of the plant being its fruit, and since the species can grow so rapidly, prohibiting the vines from growing out of control necessarily involves actively cutting them back during both the Winer, and during the growing season as well. With vigilance and care however, it is possible to train them along prepared trellises or other supports. As such, they can make a beneficial, albeit time-consuming, addition to many gardens and habitats.

Prickly Pear Cactus (*Opuntia spp.*)

Perhaps the hardiest specie, and one of the most recognizable, prickly pear cacti have a very long season in the wild. After the Spring rains have come and gone, prickly pear cacti begin sprouting their new growth for the year. As a succulent, cacti are adapted for dry or arid conditions best, so a sudden influx of water and nutrients, followed by an increasing amount of sunlight, causes them to transform their stored reserves of energy into fresh, new growth. Their new paddles begin growing in earnest in mid to late May and begin to be fully formed a month later in June.

The flowers begin to form and blossom around mid-Summer, at the end June. Endowed with the same water-preservation abilities as the rest of the plant, the prickly pear fruit have the longest season of any wild edible specie. The fruits commonly last from late August or early September until October or, on rare occasions, mid-December.

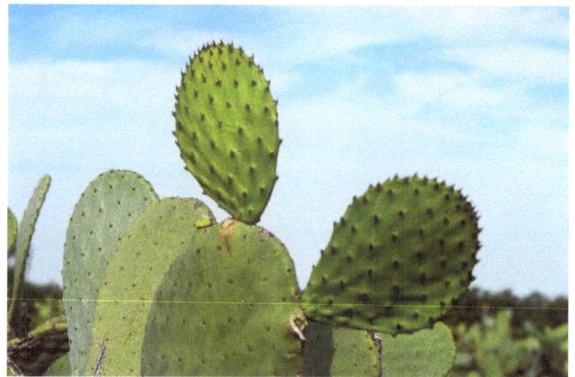

Prickly pear cactus is a succulent with large, ovoid flat pads covered in sharp spines, which are actually modified leaves. They can grow to over 6 feet tall, and if allowed will spread over entire patches of land. The fresh young pads start out with their spines covered by a soft, green cap, which they lose a couple of weeks later. Each long, sharp spine is surrounded by dozens of smaller, irritating, hair thin glochids which can easily penetrate skin and clothing and remain lodged for a considerable amount of time. The flowers which form in midsummer are generally large and bright yellow, with many over-lapping wavy petals. These flowers bloom from a thick, fleshy stem which forms into the ripe fruit after being pollinated. The fruits are lime green at first, but ripen to a deep magenta color by Autumn, and are covered by the same fine glochids as the mature paddles.

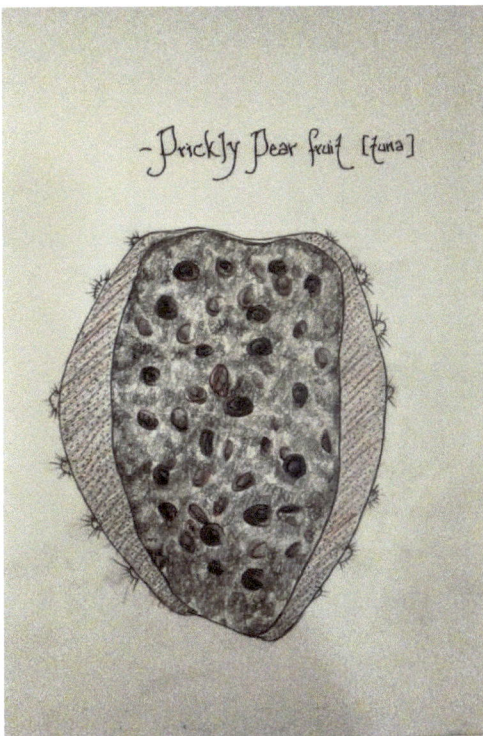

Prickly pear thrives best in arid, desert conditions, however, it can tolerate a number of environments provided its roots can remain relatively dry. Soils with a higher clay content and which retain water, or otherwise humid environments, are not ideal locations to see this species growing. In areas where it may thrive

though, prickly pear cacti can form huge colonies, and grow quite quickly.

Both the mature fruit and paddles of prickly pear cacti are edible. Cacti pads can be seen in many commercial markets labelled as nopales and are commonly used as a vegetable in a wide variety of dishes. The pads have a distinct, lemony flavor that makes them an intriguing ingredient in salad, guacamole or stir fries. The fruits can be easily juiced and turned into syrups or jellies for use in a wide variety of dessert dishes.

Prickly pears cacti are foraged by many different wildlife species. Their water retention capabilities make them an excellent source of fluids and nutrients for species in arid environments, or during drought conditions. The flowers as well are a source of nectar for many species of insect, including native bees and butterflies. To propagate these cacti, the most effective method is to remove mature paddles from established specimens and submerge, halfway, into loose sand. They may either be planted as such in pots, prepared beds, or appropriate natural locations. Provided the specimen does not become inundated with water, it will have established roots and begun producing new growth by the following Spring. If a sample is transplanted early enough in the Spring or late Winter, it is possible that it may produce new growth that same year. Prickly pear cactus is possible to propagate by seed as well, however this is an extremely unreliable and time-consuming method. The mature seeds can reliably be germinated if scattered in a desired location as soon as they ripen, however it can take several growing seasons before the young plants are large enough to produce

considerable paddles, much less flowers and fruit.

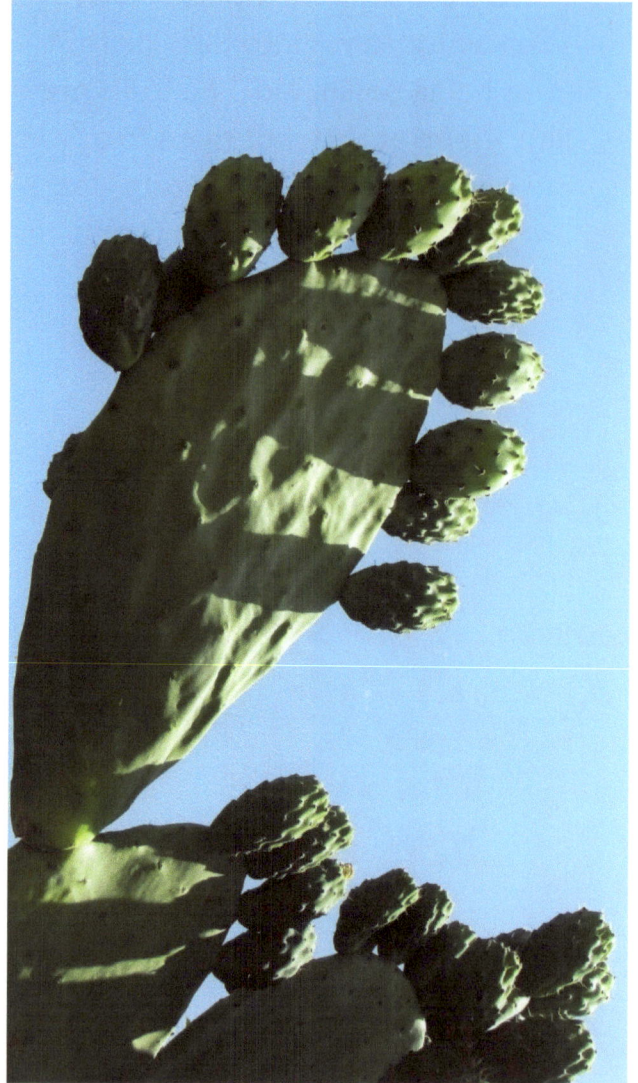

Unripened Prickly Pear Fruits

American Beautyberry
(*Callicarpa americana*)

Beautyberry season is another relatively long harvest, and one of the most anticipated species every year. American beautyberry comes into season right at the end of Summer, around the beginning of September. It begins sprouting new leaves and shoots earlier in the Spring, and during the Summer it produces its flowers. The resultant berries often last on the bush through the month of October until the beginning of November, and even though the forests around them turn cool, naked and grey, their ripe fruits still fill the woods with a bright sea of magenta.

Beautyberry is a perennial flowering shrub, which often grows to between 4 and 9 feet tall. Its leaves are large and pinnately-shaped with smooth margins. The leaves are oppositely arranged along the long, thin branches. The flowers are small, faintly pink, and appear in tight clusters at the junctures of the leaves with the main stems. Its iconic berries average about ½ an inch across, and likewise are produced in clusters at the point between the oppositely arranged leaves. The berries start out white or faint pink in color but ripen to a deep magenta or purple.

American beautyberries love well drained to sandy environments in partial shade. They are common in the understory of Eastern pine forests or well-developed post oak savannahs. It is possible for them to grow in full sun, however heavily flooded habitats are prohibitive of their growth.

Beautyberries are an excellent source of wild carbohydrates and minerals. Harvesting beautyberries is a task best suited for groups of people. In areas where they are prolific, the task of harvesting any considerable amount can seem daunting to any single individual. Additionally, in such areas, there is never any shortage of berries, and local populations are rarely in any danger from over-harvesting. Beautyberry jelly is an American folk-favorite.

Cooking, or otherwise heating the berries causes the sugars present in them to fully mature and become incredibly sweet, with a flavor reminiscent of ripened apples and spices. Due to their slight raw astringency, they have also been traditionally used as spice rubs for roasts or other meats.

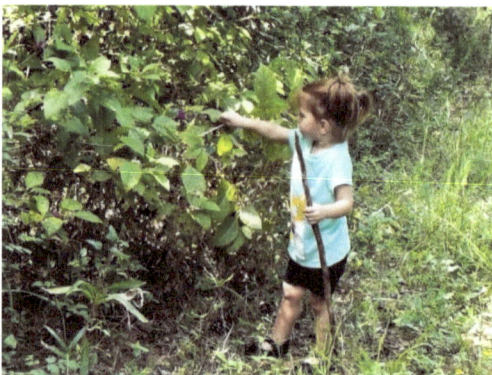

Beautyberry is an important species for white-tailed deer, as well as migratory songbirds. Because the berries may persist for so long on the branch, they are an important food source for migratory bird species before their seasonal migrations. When thinking of planting for beautyberry, the most reliable method is to take root cuttings during January or early February. Young saplings may also be transplanted in February or March. Young specimens from previous years may also be trimmed back in the Fall and re-located during the Winter, once the plants have become dormant. Sprouting from seed, with beautyberry, is extremely unreliable however.

American Lotus (*Nelumbo lutea*)

American lotus begins growing during late Spring, with the onset of the seasonal rains and rising humidity. After May ends, by early June, the plants themselves can reach between 4 – 6 feet in height. The beautiful flowers begin appearing in July to August and can usually last until September when they begin going to seed. These seed heads begin ripening by the beginning of Fall, at the end of September, but can remain on the plant well into the Winter. By December, the large, lush fronds and green stems will turn to withered, dried debris and are summarily washed away by the rains and cold, howling winds.

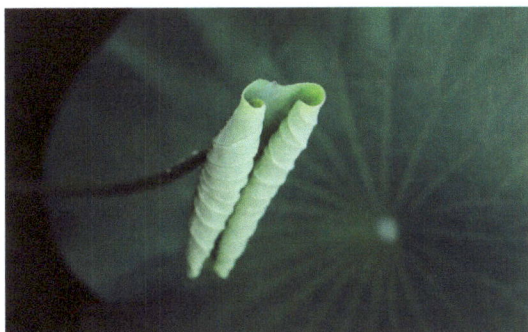

American lotus is a perennial species of flowering wetland plant. Similar in structure and appearance to the common water lily, lotus can be distinguished by its much larger form and growth habit. Opposed to the water lily, lotus fronds and flowers extend far above the surface of the water they grow out of, sometimes reaching several feet tall. The fronds themselves also are much larger than those of water lilies, and form complete circles, whereas water lilies have a characteristic "V" section cut out of them. American lotus flowers are a cream to bright yellow in color, with on average between 12 - 22 petals arranged around a central, immature seed-head. After pollination, the petals fall away, and this seed-head becomes engorged, with 10 – 20 ripe seeds being produced.

As a strictly aquatic species, lotus plants grow in still or slow-moving, shallow bodies of water. Marshes, swamps, and sheltered lake coves are all places where lotus prefers to grow. Seasonally flooded environments, or places which habitually retain water are also places where this species likes to flourish.

Lotus plants have two useful resources worth harvesting; their ripe seeds and the thick, extensive roots which spread along the bottom of the wetlands wherein they're found. Both parts of the plant begin to come into season around the same time of year as well.

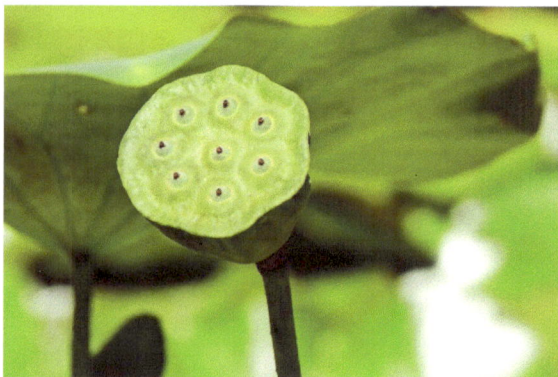

After the seeds are fully ripened, the plant begins storing nutrients and energy into its root systems in preparation for Winter, and it is at this time that the roots begin to be their most edible and delicious. The roots of the lotus can be cooked similar to many other edible roots, either similar to sweet potatoes or boiled as a cooked vegetable and

mashed as a side dish or appetizer. The seeds however need to have to inedible green germ removed from the inside of the seed before they are adequately palatable. This seed germ can be quite bitter and unpleasant to taste.

American lotus plants can provide a secure and complete habitat, much in the same manner as cattails do. The tall, emergent fronds can shelter both waterfowl and a wide variety of fish species too. The ripened seeds are eaten by both waterfowl as well as many other species of wildlife. Beavers and muskrats may also make their homes amongst the plants and make use of the rich rhizomes as nutritious source of food. Lotus plants are a wonderful addition to local environments, provided the water requirements can be met. Being such large plants, they are unsuitable for planting in either pots or containers, as they will quickly outgrow them. Should they be able to be planted close to nearby creeks or ponds, the most reliable method is to transplant portions of the rootstock from existing plants in the wild. The ripe seeds can also be collected and planted, provided their outer coat is lightly scarified first.

Commercial Lotus Roots

Pecan (*Carya illinoinensis*)

Pecans are one of the most anticipated harvests of the year, not just for humans, but for all manner of species as well. Pecan trees are slow to begin showing their new growth for the year, typically waiting until the rains have come, in April or May, to begin sprouting new leaves. The small, inconspicuous flowers appear around midsummer, and the immature fruits start to be noticeable by the end of July or August. By the beginning of Fall, at the end of September, the nuts will have finally begun to ripen, that is, if local squirrels and other impatient wildlife do not try to eat them first.

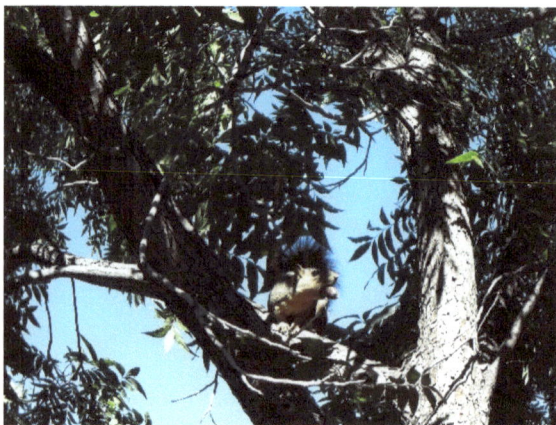

As soon as the young, green nuts emerge, fox and grey squirrels, as well as many other arboreal species, will begin devouring as many of the fruits as they can, regardless of whether they have begun to ripen or not.

A tall, deciduous tree with a rounded crown, pecan trees have grey, shaggy bark and commonly grow in excess of 100 feet tall in maturity. Their leaves are compound, with between 9 and 17 leaflets on each. These leaflets have a lanceolate shape and are finely toothed along their margins. The leaves are bright green and thin, with the late Summer sunshine easily glowing through them. The flowers are sexually dimorphic, with both male and female flowers being present on a single tree. Both male and female flowers are small, thin catkins, being on average between 3 – 5 inches in length, and yellow to lime green in color. The nuts which form after pollination are actually a form of drupe and are covered by a fleshy green husk which turns olive or brown as the fruits ripen inside.

Pecan trees prefer moist habitats with richer soils where they can still receive ample sunlight. They are a woodland canopy specie, forming an important part of forest overstories. They are also more commonly found in moist, humid bottomlands where they may receive ample water. Even locations where pools of standing water habitually form can be good environments to see pecan trees growing in.

Gathering pecans can be an enjoyable, communal experience when shared with family and friends. The extra hands can speed the collection process (although picking pecans is not difficult) and can be rewarding and very exciting, especially for young children. Large, mature trees can produce hundreds of fruits, and several bags may be filled in an hour's time by even a small group of foragers. As can be expected, the husks and shells need to be removed from the fruits before they can be eaten, but afterwards, the possibilities for these delicious nuts is limited only by the imagination.

As has been mentioned, pecan trees are an important food source for many species. They can also provide shelter for the raising of young and as a haven from predators as well.

Propagating pecan trees, as with most trees or woody species, is best accomplished by purchasing young saplings from reputable, local nurseries. Germination of pecan seeds is possible, but the chance of individual seedlings surviving to sexual maturity is extraordinarily slim. Transplanting young specimens from the wild can also be rather hazardous. The roots of trees and other woody species are prone to shock if mishandled, or if moved at the wrong time of year. Given the potential for permanent damage to an individual, it is far better to leave young trees where they have already become established, so they may continue growing into the pillars of the local environments they are destined to be, where they are found.

Autumn Equinox

"No Spring nor Summer beauty

Hath such grace as I have seen

In one Autumnal face."

-John Donne, The Complete Poetry and Selected Prose

Truly the final harvest of the year is that of life itself, and during this moon we see the annual wild hunt begin. Human hunters as well as mating deer all give chase to one another throughout the Autumnal forests. All manner of waterfowl and migratory songbirds race through the sky on their way South. By the end of this month too, the great oak trees finally ripen their acorns, and as the nighttime temperatures drop, so too do this bounty begin to fall, littering the forest floor, and fueling the wild dance under the blood red trees.

The Hunting Moon

October

Sumac (*Rhus spp.*)

In late August through mid-September, open meadows and the borders alongside sandy forests appear alive with bright red flames. These fiery fruit clusters crown the small, elegant sumac trees which have just come into season. Their flowers bloomed after the end of June, at the beginning of Summer, and have slowly ripened into the flamboyant berry clusters now available. Coming into season at roughly the same time of year as American beautyberry fruit, both sumac and beautyberries are common sights in the same environments with each other and may be gathered in concert. Sumac leaves are one of the few species which actively change color with the seasons in the South, and shortly after their fruits have ripened, they begin turning a brilliant burgundy color as well. The leaves fall soon afterwards, and the trees enter their period of dormancy for the Winter, waiting for the time when Summer will come again.

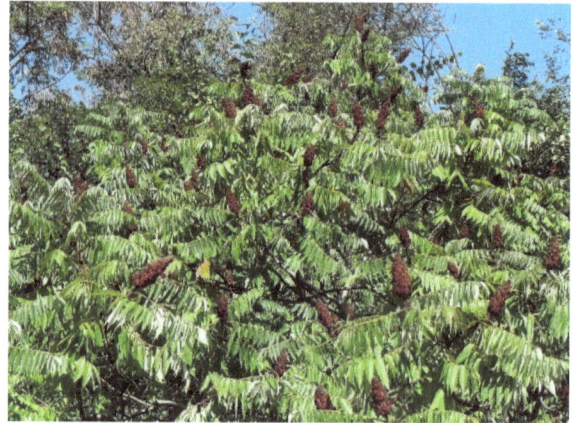

A small, deciduous tree, sumac usually never reaches more than 7 – 8 feet tall. Its bark is typically smooth, grey, and slightly mottled. The trees' trunks remain rather slim up their length, not branching out until usually 5 – 6 feet up their bodies. The slender, individual branches have a more rouged color, and diverge at a single point from the main trunk, forming a rounded crown of leaves. The leaves themselves are compound, with 11 – 17 lanceolate-shaped leaflets on each stem. These leaf blades can be decidedly serrated along their margins, with prominent pinnate venation. The flower clusters appear at the apex of the tree's crown, or at the ends of axillary branches on larger individuals. Forming dense clusters, the inflorescences are small and round, and are white or pale green to yellow in color. These flowers ripen into dense clusters of small red berries between 6 – 12 inches tall. Each small berry is about as big around as a pencil eraser and covered in a shimmering ichor which imparts a strongly tart or lemony flavor. The root systems of sumac trees are composed of adventitious rhizomes which are capable or forming dense stands in loose soils.

Sumac trees are most commonly found growing in well drained to sandy conditions, as part of a well-developed, mature understory in larger forests. In the American South, they are commonly found growing under pine forests, as these typically form on sandy soils and have plenty of room under their canopies to allow

sunlight and permit other species to grow and flourish. Sumac trees can also be found growing along the borders of mature forests or even across open meadows, provided the areas are undisturbed and well drained. Environments which habitually experience fires are another common place to find this species thriving.

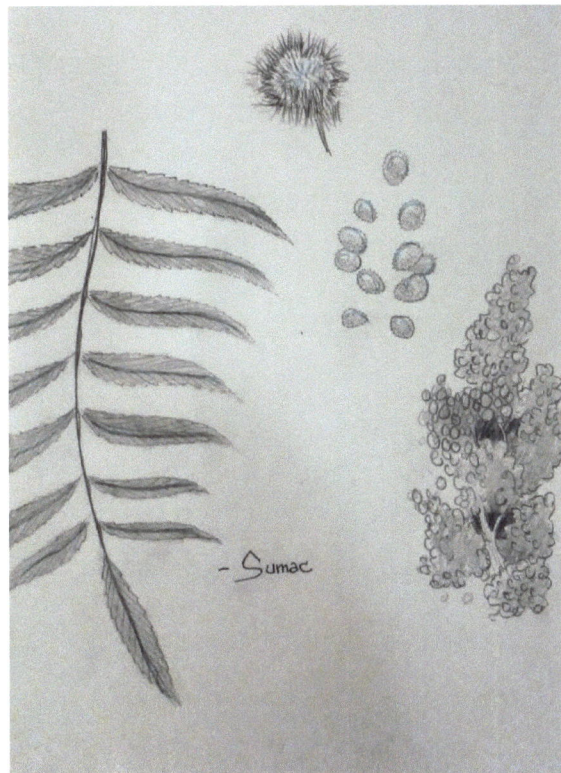

- Sumac

Sumac trees have relatively shallow root systems and their slender trunks and branches may be easily broken or uprooted if they are treated carelessly. When harvesting bunches of sumac berries, using a ladder when necessary to reach the apex of the trees' crowns can help avoid such damage. The tart berries are a wonderful seasoning for many different dishes, and can also be used to steep a sweet, delicious beverage. By adding several berry clusters to a pitcher of water, and letting soak overnight, a delicious drink can be made. Sumac berries are a favorite among many species of wildlife as well, and so it is important to be conscious of this need when harvesting the berries and never take more than is needed or may be realistically used.

their shallow rhizomes. As an adventitious species, active management may be necessary of planted sumac trees to ensure they do not form thick stands and crowd out any species which might grow underneath them.

Harvested Sumac Berries

As it is such a small species of tree, sumac is one woody species which it is possible to relocate reliably, should young specimens be found early enough in the year and their life cycle as well. Seedlings or small saplings can be transplanted if they are moved before any flower buds have begun to form, and care is taken with

Sparkleberry (*Vaccinium arboreum*)

Sparkleberries[15]

Once Fall arrives, the ripe fruits of the farkle or sparkleberry plant come into season. These berries can persist on the bushes for many months, on rare occasions lasting until early December. Another specie whose leaves turn color with the changing of the seasons, reddening farkleberry leaves act as a signal that the fruits have come into season too. Their small, elegant flowers bloom at the beginning of Summer, and over the next several months, the resulting fruits begin to ripen. Once the weather begins to turn cold, at the beginning of November, the fruits begin to shrivel, and the reddening leaves begin to drop from the plants.

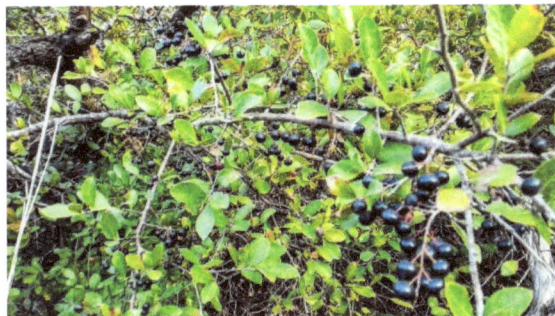

Either a large bush, or a small tree, sparkleberry is in the same genus as cranberries and blueberries. The tallest of the genus, it has a short trunk and likewise short, crooked branches. Growing on average to about 12 feet tall, its bark is grey, and somewhat scaly, and can be seen exfoliating from the trunk and branches in places. The leaves are small and elliptical, turning reddish brown with the coming of Winter. Sparkleberry leaves have a passing resemblance to those of yaupon holly, but are smooth, instead of scalloped around their margins. Sparkleberry bushes on a whole have a similar appearance to yaupon too, but have a more upright growth habit instead of the sprawling, domineering nature of the yaupon species. The flowers of sparkleberries are small, white and bell shaped. They grow, alternately arranged, along thin, tender green stems which hang from the youngest branches of the bush. The fruits that follow are similar in shape and size to domestic blueberries, although much darker in color. During their season, sparkleberry shrubs may be filled with hundreds of the delicious, juicy fruits.

Sparkleberry Tree[16]

Due to its small stature, it is essentially an understory species, but is rarely seen growing in dense forests. Sparkleberries prefer sunlight and open space to full or partial shade. They are most often found along the borders of larger woodlands, or more likely, across open savannahs. Sparkleberry likes to grow in well drained to rocky soils. The species can endure some seasonal flooding, but areas which retain water or are very clay rich, can prohibit the specie's success. Sandy, rocky hillsides or amidst native grasslands and post oak savannahs, are all excellent habitats wherein to expect to see this species.

Ripe Berries[17]

Sparkleberries are easily harvested, and may be enjoyed fresh, straight off the branch. Those berries which are the largest and ripen in partial shade have the sweetest flavor, but cooked into jam or syrups, they are all delicious.

Sparkleberries are, as is to be expected, a popular food source for many species. Migratory songbirds preparing for journeys South, and arboreal mammals readying for Winter's sleep, all make use of the long-lasting fruits. From the specie's proclivity for rocky and loose soils, it can have a mitigating effect as far as possible erosion may be concerned. Planting for sparkleberry bushes may be problematic however. As a woody specie, germination from seed carries little guarantee of success, and to propagate by root cuttings can damage the parent shrub, with still no guarantee of the cutting reaching maturity. Finding specimens at local, reputable nurseries is the best option possible. However, the species may not be common at many nurseries, except those specializing in native flora.

Small saplings or large seedlings in the wild can possibly be re-located in late Winter or early Spring, if severe caution is taken to keep as many of the fine root hairs intact. Once moved, the plant will need considerable attention, watering and soil amendment to ensure it survives the year. Any specimen which lasts until the following growing season however, has a considerably higher chance of living a long, full life.

Goldenrod (*Solidago spp.*)

Perhaps the last flower to blossom every year, goldenrod flowers burst into color after the Autumnal equinox, in early to mid-October. Immature goldenrod plants are rather nondescript, and generally unnoticed until their radiant flowers bloom. They begin growing, along with many other species, in mid to late May, after the seasonal Spring rains have ended. In the humid air, they can reach up to several feet tall as they stretch towards the sun. They continue to grow until late Summer and September comes, when they begin sprouting their immature flower buds. Once the nights begin to lose their heat, and most other species have passed away or gone to seed, their bright flowers explode as a beautiful reminder to life amidst the browning landscape.

Goldenrod is a tall flowering perennial in the large *Asteraceae* family. It spreads and forms large stands by adventitious rhizomes in the early Spring. By May and June, the young plants have begun to shoot upwards along tall, inch thick stalks, reaching on average between 3 – 5 feet in height. The leaves are long, lanceolate and can be smooth or show slight teeth along their margins.

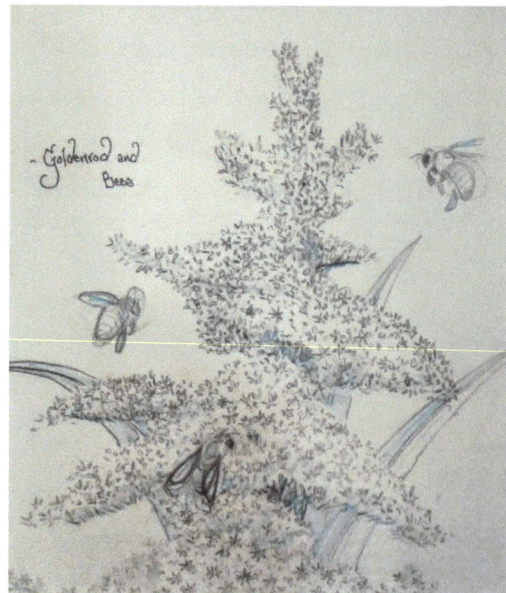

They are arranged in a whorled pattern up the tall stem. As the plant reaches its apex, it may branch out several times, with all stems continuing to point upwards. The flowers which appear later are small and bright yellow in color. They are pistillate and are composed of both ray and disc florets. After pollination, the flowers close, and re-open and the white-haired seeds are carried away on the winds.

A decidedly sun-loving species, goldenrod grows almost exclusively in full sunlight. Goldenrod can tolerate some seasonal inundation, but soils which retain water for long periods of time can prohibit the spread of the creeping rhizomes which produce the tall stalks. For its propensity to form large colonies, it is not easily crowded out by other eager, herbaceous species or native grasses either. It can be occasionally seen growing in large, open meadows amongst woodlands too. However, it never quite reaches the same height nor prolific flowerings as it does across open prairies and savannah.

When harvesting goldenrod flowers, it is best to cut entire branches, with all the attached flowers intact, and to separate them out afterwards. Attempting to pluck handfuls of flowers from off the plant can result in unwarranted damage to the remaining flowers. Traditionally, the plant has been used as a medicinal herb to treat kidney or bladder inflammation and dried goldenrod flowers make a wonderful tea. Both the fresh flowers, as well as the young, immature leaves may be gathered. Their flavor is very like anise or licorice and has a slightly astringent nature. Because of this, they may also be used as a seasoning for roasts or in other dishes as well.

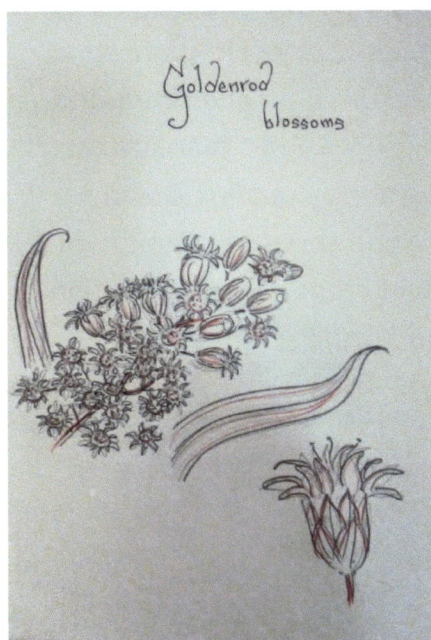

Though commonly accused of inciting hay fevers and aggravating allergies, the flowers of goldenrod possess very little pollen. The Autumnal maladies they are usually thought to cause are actually caused by the concurrently blooming ragweed. The flowers of goldenrod species are a boon to nearly every species of pollinator, as they appear just before they are due to begin hibernation or embark on their migrations South for the Winter. To propagate them, sections of the rhizomes may be unearthed and transplanted in prepared garden beds. The mature seeds can be gathered as well, but due to their small size, collecting and planting them may prove a tedious task. Mature goldenrod plants can spread rather well, and will certainly fill up any sunny beds they are planted in. For this reason, it is recommended that steps be taken to manage their growth, either by putting down barriers to the spread of their roots, or by actively removing young plants during the Spring.

"Listen! The wind is rising,

    And the air is wild with leaves,

        We have had our Summer evenings,

           Now for October eves!"

-Humbert Wolfe

The leaves are finally falling, turning the beautiful forests all the colors of the rainbow before they disappear. After the rut ends, the deer will all crouch antlerless in the gray Winter woods, having shed the crowns they spent all the long, warm months growing. We also call this month the Fur Moon, because all hibernating mammals will have grown in their thick Winter coats in preparation for the coming cold. Truly Winter is coming. Whether a time of preparation or one last wild fling, soon all will endure the icy stillness, either by the hand of Death or long, slow sleep.

The Falling Moon

November

Acorn (*Quercus spp.*)

After the beginning of Fall, in October and November, as the deer begin heatedly giving each other chase, the rich fruits of the great oak trees ripen and begin to litter the ground. The oak trees began flowering for the year around midsummer or in early July. The nuts themselves become visible around the end of Summer, in September, however they are usually hidden behind the mass of foliage. It is not until the large leaves begin to drop, that their exact number can easily be seen. Though they may be ripe, they do not readily begin dropping to the ground in any large number until the weather turns decidedly colder. This is usually by November, but in warm years, or in the far South, they may hang on the naked branches well until December. The last great feast of the year, such a profuse abundance of energy and nutrients provides life and

nourishment to not only the rutting deer, but to nearly every other herbivorous species of wildlife committed to enduring the Winter months rather than flee to the South.

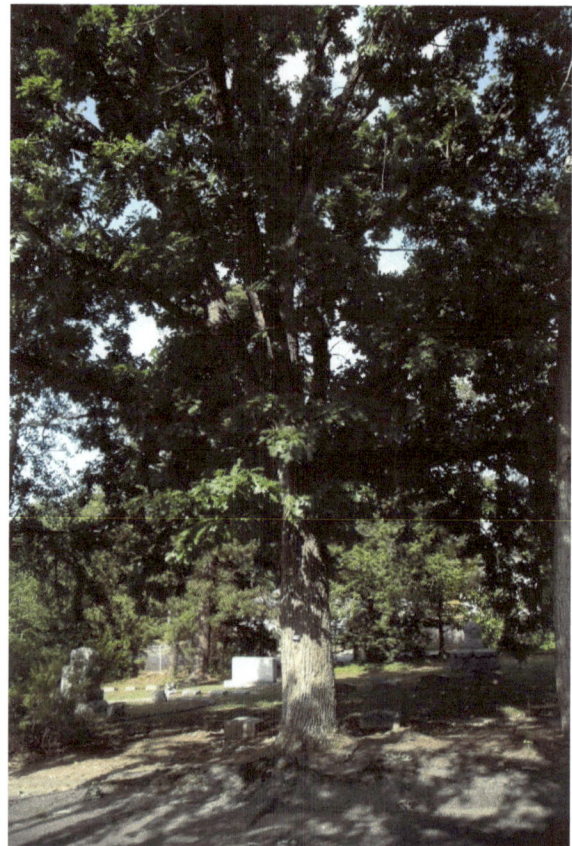

Bur Oak[18]

Oak trees are easily recognizable for their fruit, the acorns, but also for their massive size and large, deeply lobed leaves. The species are commonly divided between red and white oak species, but it is the fruit of the white oak varieties which are the better for harvesting. Red oak trees have a higher concentration of bitter tasting tannins which must be removed before the nuts are palatable, while white oak varieties can have very little or none. Red oak trees have leaves which regularly come to points at their tips and include the evergreen varieties as well. White oak leaves are usually larger, with rounded tips to their leaves, all of which are deciduous. Of the white oak varieties, the fruit of the bur oak, *Quercus macrocarpa,* are the largest, with little bitter tannins present and are common throughout much of the Eastern United States. Their acorns can be up to 5 inches in their caps, with the nuts themselves being still several inches long and wide. The nuts are pale yellow to cream colored inside and are generally smooth with slight wrinkles.

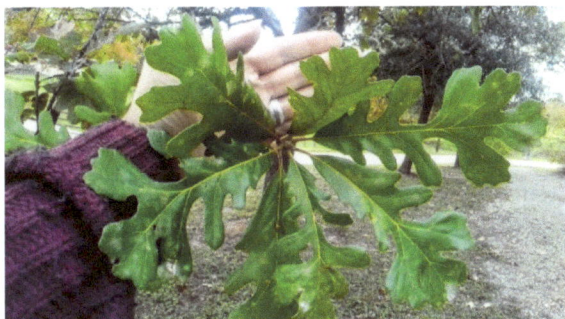

Oak trees are bottomland species, preferring habitats which are more moist with richer soils. The roots of many oak species are quite shallow, and so drier, well drained or sandy environments can make them more susceptible to prolonged or severe droughts. Where they are found, mature oak trees naturally dominate the landscape, becoming the pillars of their communities and creating micro-habitats all of their own. Towering over all other species, they soak up the full sun and can spread out nearly as wide as they are tall.

Not all oak varieties produce nuts every year, but the years in which they do, they can cover the earth around them with their fruits. Acorns provide an immense source of calories and carbohydrates and are well suited for turning into flour for baking. They may also be candied or turned into a nut spread as well. Before they can be eaten though, the nuts will need to be leached of any tannins. They may be boiled, in several changes of water, but this method removes much of the nutritious oils and lipids from the nuts. More easily, they can be submerged in water-filled jars and refrigerated, with the water being changed out once or twice a day. With either method, grinding the nuts before leaching makes the process much faster by nearly half. White oak varieties, naturally, take much less time to leach than red oaks, but either variety results in a rich, slightly sweet food source.

Oak trees are the backbone of many ecosystems, providing food, shelter and a complete habitat for wildlife, much in the same way as the cattail. They secure their soils and mitigate erosion, as well as helping to trap moisture in the soil, under the spread of their shading branches and between their great roots.

Oak trees are popular candidates in landscaping throughout the United States, and so are easily found at nearly every nursery. As with other large, woody species, specimens sprouted from seed have little chance of surviving to adulthood. Additionally, it is inadvisable to try transplanting sections cut from mature rootstock, a this can damage the shallow root systems of the parent tree and give no greater guarantee of the specimen growing to maturity. Healthy saplings from reputable nurseries are by far the most effective method for propagating the species. Care should be taken when planting for new trees though, with an eye to the future and how the tree will grow and take up space. Ensuring it has plenty of room to spread and fill out, is both good for the young tree and will give the best benefit to the surrounding landscape.

Hackberry (*Celtis laevigata*)

A mostly ignored or maligned species, the humble hackberry ripens its sweet, delicious seeds and comes into season during November, and the seeds may remain on the tree well into January at times. The flowers which bloom during mid to late Summer often go entirely unnoticed. The immature fruits, as they ripen throughout the Fall, are also almost invisible until the tree's leaves fall, and the fruits turn bright red.

Hackberry trees are fast-growing and relatively short-lived trees, which commonly grow along the edges of lowland forests. Though not as tall as other species, their trunks are very long and straight. Their bark is pale grey and slightly mottled, and as they age, they become increasingly covered in woody bumps and warts. Their branches are rather slender and long, often reaching almost halfway back down their long trunks. Because their wood is so soft, their limbs often easily break during strong storms, littering the ground around them. Their thin leaves are pinnate and slightly curved, about 4 – 6 inches long on average, and alternately arranged along the tree's stems. Their flowers are small, round and pale green to white in color. Both male and female flowers exist on the same tree. The fruits which follow are a bright green, but slowly ripen to a dark red throughout the Fall.

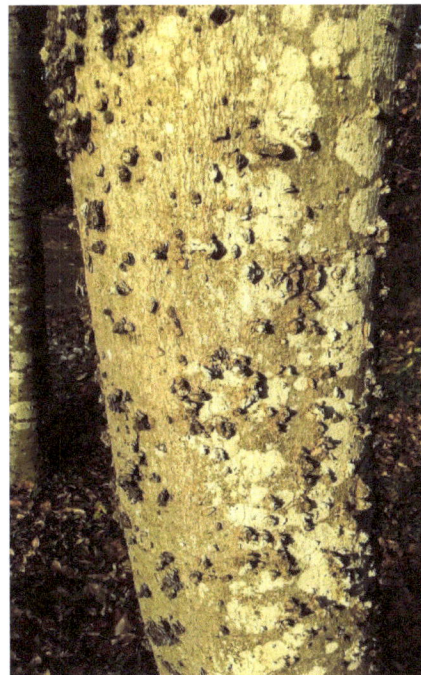

Hackberry trees generally form part of the upper canopy of the forests wherein they are found. They generally prefer to grow in moist woodlands which may experience seasonal flooding, or which retain moisture throughout the year. As they are a fast-growing species, and because they have a shorter lifespan than many other trees, they are more commonly seen growing near the edges of forest, rather than their center.

Hackberries were once one of the most important food sources for humans around the world. Perhaps the oldest known foraged food, evidence of people gathering hackberries for food dates back at least 500,000 years. Gathering hackberries can be tedious work though; the berries are small, and grow singularly along the trees branches, making it impossible to gather them in bunches. For this fact, and for the sheer enjoyment of the experience, it is best to gather hackberries in a group. The more people foraging together, the more quickly a large amount of seeds may be collected, and the shared activity can bring a tone of celebration to the grey Winter season. The small seeds are high in fructose, and rich in

protein and essential fats. Hackberries may be extremely sweet but are rather hard. The best way to enjoy them is to crush them into a coarse meal first. They may be powdered, as an additive for baking, or formed into trail bars for snacking. They may also be crushed and then boiled, to produce a sweet "milk", which is a most delicious drink.

Hackberries are an important food source for wildlife, due to their ability to offer food long after other species have become bare. The trees are also hosts for a variety of larval pollinator species during the Spring. Hackberry trees spread by seed but can also spread by cut branches and stems. If rooting hormone is used, sprouting cut, young branches can be an effective and economic means of sprouting new trees. Due to the trees fast growth habit, and abundance of broken and falling limbs, this method may be both expedient and painless for the gardener, and for the tree as well. Hackberry trees are not commonly seen in most nurseries; however, it is planted as a windbreak on agricultural properties, and companies which cater to agri-businesses can have saplings available for sale occasionally.

During this time of year, the owls begin calling to each other in the cold darkness, staking claim to territory and love in the midst of the world's repose. Alternately a symbol of death and hidden knowledge, owls have always had an unnerving connotation for human cultures the world over. During the depths of Winter, there can be no more apt icon for the state of life around us. The cold, bleak landscape, the quiet broken only by the haunted hooting of one silent winged hunter to another. Yet in truth, these creatures are already preparing for the coming of the new year, and once the solstice turns again, night will indeed begin to fade. Winter is the shortest of all seasons, and though it may inspire fear and doubt, life is quick to return and is dependable in its promise. Perhaps this is the true secret the owls guard, and hint towards, as they call to each other in the night.

Wapato (*Sagittaria spp.*)

Wapato Plant[19]

Arrowhead, or wapato, plants are one of the first, rich tubers to be gathered at the end of the year. Having sprouted their leaves in the Spring, flowered during the Summer months, and finally gone to seed by Autumn, the plants restore all remaining nutrients to their roots and become dormant for the coming Winter by December.

Wapato is genus of flowering, wetland plants, best recognized by their large, arrowhead-shaped leaves. These leaves unfurl during the Spring from long, inch thick stalks, emanating from a central root mass. Each leaf has three pointed lobes, two extending downwards, the third pointing up. The leaves have parallel venation, reaching from the point where the stem joins to the ends of each of the three lobes. The flowers bloom along a stalk which sprouts from the center of the plant. Each flower has 3 – 5 medium-sized white petals, with yellow or pink to dark purple centers. These flowers result in small, round, green fruits which turn brownish and begin to shrivel as they ripen on the stalk. The plant's roots form large, rich bulbs at their tips. These bulbs are commonly several inches across; about the size of an average golf ball. They are covered by a thin, brownish outer skin, but are cream colored inside. These bulbs can form new plants which can result in large stands of the plant forming across a single area.

Wapato plants are strictly aquatic, and favor growing in shallow, still or slow-moving waters. They are commonly seen in marshes, swamps, and other wetland areas which are covered by water year-round.

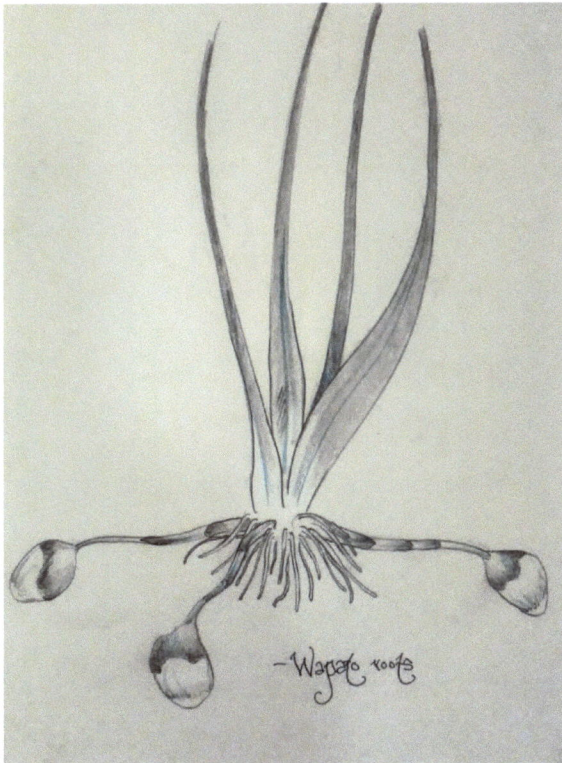

As they are submerged beneath mud and water, and usually available during the colder months of the year, foraging for wapato bulbs can be unappealing. The task is made easier by wearing tall waders and making use of thin, long-handled shovels to unearth the tubers. Finding the bulbs or tubers can still take some searching, and it is this which can take the most time. With proper attire and patience however, the effort spent is greatly rewarded. Wapato bulbs are rich in energy and nutrients and exceptionally easy to prepare. Their brown, outer skins removed, they may be cooked in any method as a domestic potato would,

having a slightly nutty flavor similar to sweet potatoes.

Wapato Tubers[20]

Several wildlife species, including beavers and muskrats, will eat the rich rhizomes of the species. Ducks and other waterfowl may also feed on the ripe seeds during the Fall. As they can form thick stands, the plants have the ability to offer shelter to many species of aquatic wildlife, from frogs to small fish species. Propagating wapato plants is easily accomplished by re-planting some of the harvested root bulbs in pots or containers with water, or in small ponds. Even though the plant has adventitious roots, the harvesting of these for food is excellent for keeping the plant from spreading and crowding out other species. Like other wetland species, it does have a high-water requirement, and without available waters to plant them in, the task of providing water for them can become tedious and inefficient. Due to their rich, submerged bulbs, the plant is able to tolerate some drying, but like canna lilies, it is advised that they should be planted where they can remain adequately moist.

Bull nettle (*Cnidoscolus stimulosus*)

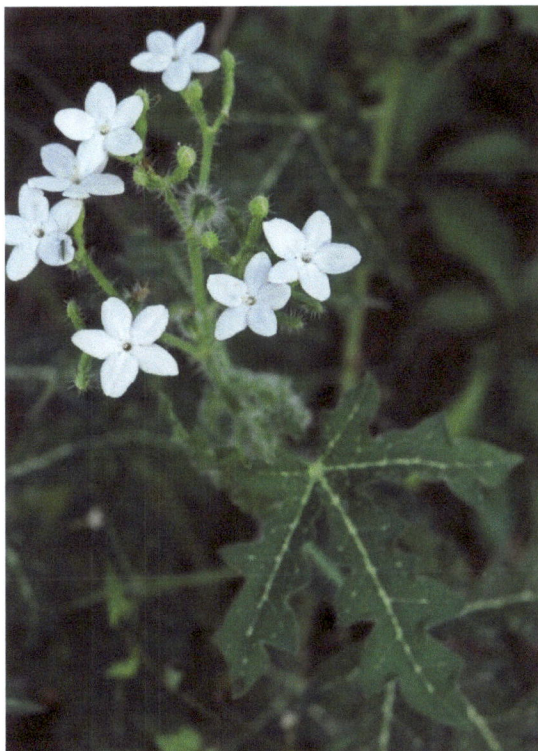

Bull Nettle[21]

One of the largest roots available, bull nettle roots are swollen rich with energy and nutrients by Winter, and once the coldest weather arrives, all their stored starches begin being converted into sweet sugars. Bull nettle begins showing new growth by April and shortly after, by May or June, the plants begin flowering. The large seed capsules begin ripening by late August to early September, after which the plant returns to a state of dormancy for the Winter. During this time, it shunts as much of the available nutrients as possible into its large taproot for the following year.

Bull nettle is a perennial plant that, as the name implies, is covered in hypodermic stinging hairs. It has a sprawling growth habit, and rarely reaches more than 2 – 3 feet in eight. Its large leaves are alternately arranged along its stems and are deeply lobed, having either 3 or 5 fingers on each. In the late Spring and early Summer, it produces small, five petaled white flowers which are extremely fragrant. These are quickly pollinated and begin ripening into medium sized seedpods, also covered in stinging hairs. They are divided into sections internally, containing a total of five seeds. The mature seedpods start out a verdant green, changing to a light brown as they age and dry out. Eventually they pop open, expelling the large seeds inside. The large, edible, taproot is light to mottled brown in color and has a somewhat rough or bumpy texture on the outside. The taproot can be quite large, at around 3 – 4 feet in length, often exceeding the above ground portions of the plant in size.

Bull nettle is commonly found on sandy hillsides or in open forest meadows. It prefers light, well drained soils with plenty of sunshine, however it is rarely found across open prairies. Along the edges of sandy pine forests, or in the clearings amongst oak savannah are excellent places to expect to find this species. It is also possible to find it growing as a colonizer amongst abandoned or reclaimed areas of land, either in abandoned lots or construction sites in urban areas or old farm steads outside of towns.

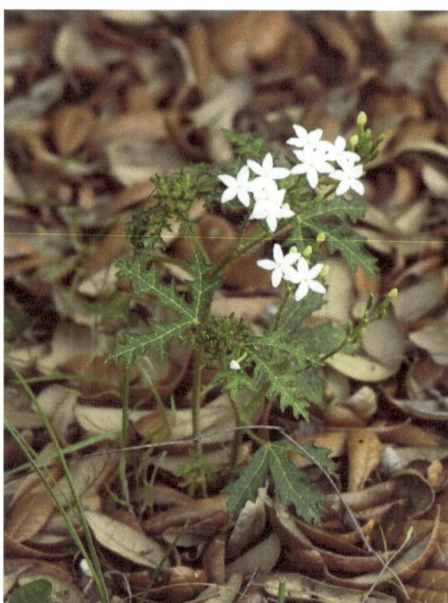

Young Bull Nettle[22]

As with other stinging species, care should be taken when handling and harvesting bull nettle plants in order to avoid the painful stings. The large taproot can be dug up once the above ground portions of the plant are removed. To harvest the entire root, a hole roughly 3 feet deep should be dug about 6 – 12 inches

from the base of the plant, and then the soil around the root carefully removed. Bull nettle roots can be used much in the same way as yams or potatoes are. A more dense, fibrous core runs through the center of the roots and should be removed after cooking. The large, nutritious roots have a flavor similar to starchy nuts or pasta and are excellent seasoned with cinnamon or other spices such as basil or oregano. They can be boiled or roasted in the oven, or even in coals of a campfire, and mashed or diced and added to other dishes.

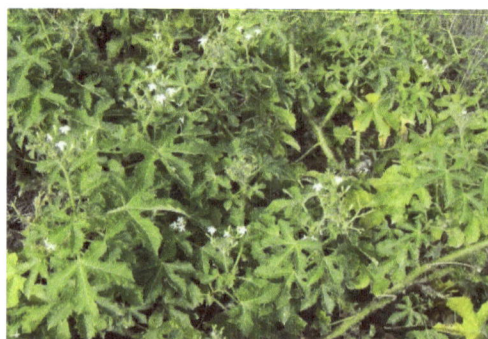

Mature Bull Nettle[23]

Bull nettle, with its fragrant blossoms, is particularly attractive to pollinators, including butterflies and bees, but also some bird species. The ripe seeds are edible and sought after by many wildlife species, including mourning doves and Rio Grande turkeys, among others. Being drought tolerant, the species is especially useful in xeriscaping and water wise or native plant landscaping. Due to its large taproot and sprawling large leaves, bull nettle can also be useful in mitigating erosion in barren or denuded areas. When planting for bull nettle, the large, ripe seeds usually offer the simplest means of propagation. Root cuttings, especially in Winter, or young plant seedlings may also be transplanted. However, care should be taken to not damage fine root hairs or young plants, and the harmful spines may already be present as well.

Gayfeather (*Liatris spicata*)

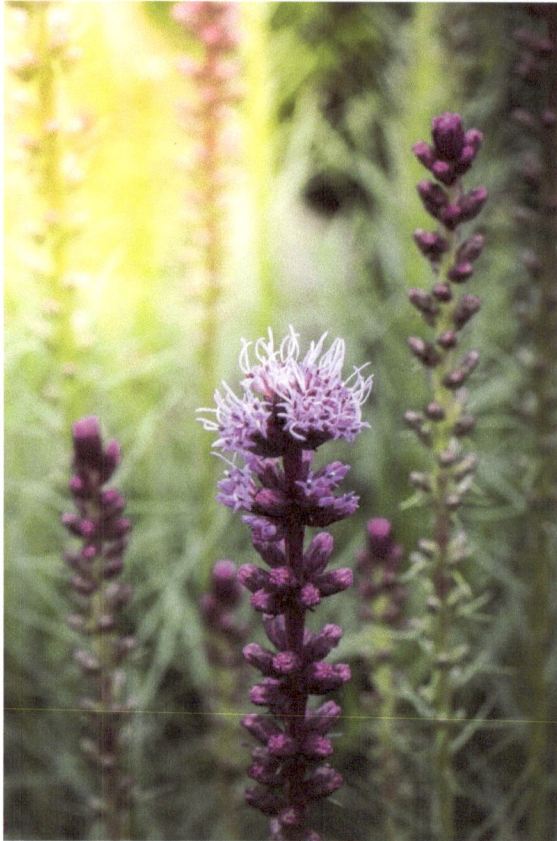

Another delicious root vegetable, Liatris or gayfeather comes into season just as all above ground plants have become dormant and the weather begun to turn cold. Gayfeather roots are usually small, about the size of a large wild onion bulb or small golf ball, and fibrous. However, they quickly become palatable once the plant finishes its growth cycle for the year and transfers its remaining nutrients and energy back into its root bulb. As Winter progresses, these bulbs will become larger as they start to transform their stores of starches into sugars and start expanding in preparation for the coming year. Young gayfeather shoots begin growing in earnest in late Spring (late April-May) and by early Summer they may be ready to bloom its fantastic flower head. These beautiful, tall blooms can last well into Autumn, but by the time the American beautyberry plants have ripened in September, gayfeather blooms will have begun to dry out and their stems turn brown with age. The showy flower stalks mark their locations well, and by the time they begin to wilt, the underground root bulbs will be almost ready to pick.

Gayfeather is a perennial herb which is best recognized for its brilliant, tall flower stalk which blooms in mid to late Summer. The tall flower spikes are typically bright purple to lavender in color and resemble thin, many rayed bottle brushes. The young, green leaves are thin and sprout in a whorled pattern up the unbranched stalks. Gayfeather, like wild onions or other similar species, tends to form dense stands in good conditions.

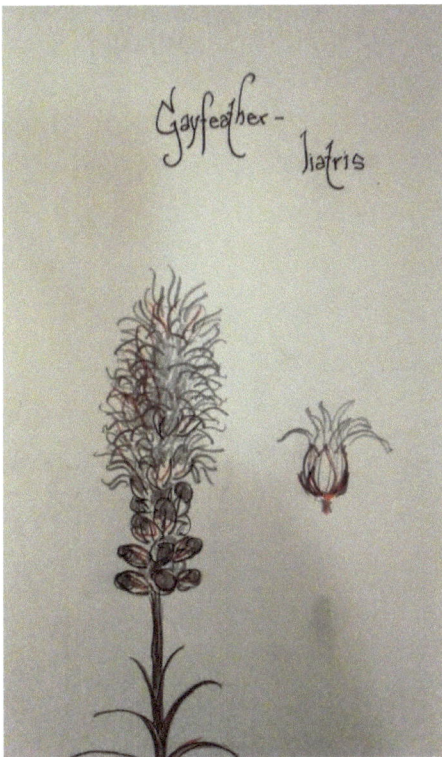

Gayfeather - liatris

Gayfeather prefers to grow in deep, moist but well drained soils. It is susceptible to root rot, so soils which have a higher content of sand and drain well are more suitable than those which retain water or experience seasonal flooding. It usually likes to live near woodlands with an open understory where they can receive ample sunlight. Like bull nettle, and many other herbaceous species, gayfeather fares better along the edges of forests rather than in full

prairie environments. This is due partially to the richer soils, but also because of reduced competition from grasses.

Harvesting gayfeather is simple, once the plant is located. After the tall flower stalks go to seed and wither in the Fall, it can be difficult to locate them during the Winter when the root bulbs are ready for picking. Many times, the withered flower stalk will remain standing, thus marking the plant's location. Other times, however, nearby landmarks or markers will have to be identified, or placed, to re-locate the plants. Gayfeather bulbs can be eaten just like potatoes. They can be roasted in the oven or boiled and mashed as an appetizer or side dish. Care should be taken when roasting though, as they can dry out and become fibrous if left in the oven too long. Gayfeather roots' small to medium size and mild flavor makes them very approachable and ideal as a way to add some wild flair to a dinner with friends.

Gayfeather is an excellent attractant for pollinator species. Species which frequent this plant include monarch butterflies, tiger swallowtails, clouded and orange sulphurs, and painted ladies. It is also attractive to several species of bee, including digger, long horned, leaf cutting, and bumblebees. They have even been seen to attract hummingbirds on occasion. The larval forms of several pollinator species also feed on the plant, including the bleeding flower, or liatris moth, whose larvae feed almost exclusively on gayfeather species. Several species of small herbivorous mammals, such as rabbits and voles, also enjoy feeding on the plant. Propagating gayfeather is best accomplished by transplanting their root bulbs during the Winter when they are active. When harvesting several roots for dinner, simply save a few to plant as a way to say thank you.

<u>Winter Solstice</u>

"In the depths of Winter

I finally learned that

Within me there lay an invincible Summer."

-Albert Camus

In Conclusion

As foragers, it is important to understand that there is a duty to protect and nurture the resources which we come to enjoy and depend on. As human beings, it is our duty to pass on this knowledge, to other individuals and to future generations. Teaching other people about these resources and how to propagate them does not just ensure an increasing supply of wild foods which can be harvested, it also helps to restore local habitat and improve the health of our environment.

When teaching others, it is important to remember the basic rules of foraging, with an emphasis on positively identifying species. This is especially important when there are potentially toxic species which can easily be confused for the species being presented. In many cases, should the "look-alike" species be extraordinarily dangerous, or be overly close in appearance, it may be worthwhile to avoid discussing the original, useful species altogether.

Foraging is meant to be a group exercise and is the perfect opportunity to bring communities of people together. Gathering handfuls of wild edibles is best enjoyed when done with friends, and the shared experience helps to reinforce what is being learned. Our minds are amazingly predisposed to retaining information regarding finding food, but the memory of pleasant times spent with other is what will keep us coming back for more.

My hope for this book has ultimately been to inspire people. To see how simple and enjoyable foraging can be and how it can impact our daily lives. But also, to give people a tangible reason to care about their local environments, and natural habitat in general. Humans are as much a part of the natural world as any other species. We are important parts of our local ecosystems, and no environment where we are found is truly complete without us. The first time you step outside, even in your own backyard, with the intent of stooping to investigate or harvest some of the little weeds which flourish there, if you listen closely, you can hear them whisper, "Welcome back!"

Our ability to positively impact our environment is a gift we share with many other forms of life in our world. Indeed, all life developed to have such a net, beneficial impact. These skills and aptitudes have not been lost in us but seeing how they can help to restore our natural world today can help us to remember what they are for. More importantly, it can help us to remember that we belong here too. Perhaps that is the greatest gift I would like to share through this book. A sense of worth and inspiration, but also of community and home.

Appendix

~Wild Flours~

Many of our favorite dishes with our wild harvests have used flour created from several of the species we collect. To aid in the enjoyment of these foods, the steps for processing those harvests into flours for cooking have been included in this appendix.

Mesquite flour

Mesquite flour is probably the easiest flour to process. Mesquite trees are also rather over-abundant in this part of Texas, and each tree can produce hundreds, if not thousands, of beans. So, they are not hard to find, nor will anyone begrudge you taking them. You may actually be doing someone a favor.

Mesquite beans have a starchy pith inside that tastes similar to sweet honey or molasses. It is rich in fructose as well as protein, so it can provide energy for hours and be incredibly filling.

Take ripe, dry beans and simply snap them up into smaller pieces and toss them into a blender or another grinder such as a grain mill.

Grind them up as you would a bunch of ice, pulsing until all of the pieces have been ground up. Then, using a mesh sieve, sift out the finely ground flour from the chaff of the outer pods and the stone hard seeds. This remnant can either be poured back into the blender to be re-ground, or used for making jelly and then added to a compost pile.

There is a wide variety of recipes you can make using mesquite bean flour, from pancakes and waffles to **pie crusts** and breads. Ensure any beans gathered are fully ripened and dry (can be pulled off the branch easily and snap in half) and do not have any black or dark mold growing on them. In extremely wet years, in places where it is humid, the rain and the bugs can combine to ruin a mesquite harvest. Luckily, other species, such as American beautyberry, typically thrive in those times.

Beautyberry flour

Once identified, the wonderful **beautyberry bush**, is not easily forgotten and it will seem to appear everywhere. It is popular in landscaping due to its natural hardiness and lack of maintenance. It also is important for local wildlife as it provides Winter forage, when many other foods are gone.

A source of wild carbohydrates, they can taste mildly astringent when raw. But, once heat is applied, the sugars inside fully mature and the berries become quite sweet. Beautyberry breads are rather light and fluffy with a decidedly rich, chocolate taste.

To make this amazing flour, simply gather as much beautyberries as possible. Puree the berries in a blender with a little water and then transfer this slurry to a dehydrator and leave on medium low until the berry puree is brittle and dry.

Afterwards, remove the dried berry puree and place in a food processor or similar grinder, and grind it until it is a fine powder.

Beautyberry flour can be stored it in any plastic or other container, but it is recommended that it be stored in a refrigerator, due to the sugars present.

Beautyberry flour is great for making brownies, cakes, **muffins**, even a seasonal Yule log or cookies.

Acorn flour

Processing acorn flour is more complicated than either mesquite or beautyberry flour, but still relatively simple.

First, crack the acorns open and chop the meat up into smaller pieces. Then toss them into the blender, just like making mesquite flour, and grind them up. It helps to add some water to the blender, to ensure they grind up easily. Next take the slurry mix and pour it into a large glass jar; an old, glass pickle jar will do perfectly. This jar is where making acorn flour takes the longest. Let the ground up acorns sit in the jar in your refrigerator and leach their bitterness into the water. Every day, pour out the coffee colored water in the jar and re-fill with fresh water from the tap. Give the jar a good shake to mix things back up and replace back in the refrigerator.

This process, depending on the type of acorns, can take a few days, to a week or longer. The acorn meal is done leaching once the flour no longer tastes bitter. Generally, "white" oaks are less bitter and take much less time, while "red" oaks can take much longer.

After the flour is done leaching, pour it through a cheese cloth or other clean rag to squeeze the water out and place in either a dehydrator or on a cookie sheet in the oven at the lowest temperature to dry. Once dried, place in a blender or other grinder to bring to a fine, floury consistency.

Although acorn flour can take some time, acorns are full of protein and healthy oils and fats. Preserving these oils into the final flour by using this cold-leaching method allows these oils to act like a binder when making acorn **pancakes** or **pizza** or muffins or any other delicious baked goods.

Image Credits

About the Author

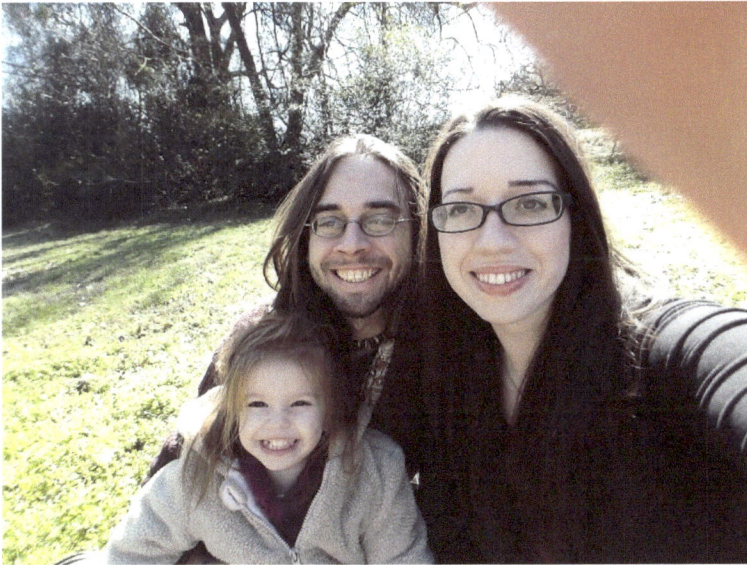

Our family has been foraging for wild foods for many years, and most of the foods we eat directly come from our local environment. Wild foods are extremely nutritious, and maintenance free. They need no supplemental watering, or fertilizer, or pesticides in order to grow healthy and strong. As important parts of their local environments, they also provide food and shelter for wildlife, as well as essential ecosystem services. Learning to use and propagate these species does not just provide a source of free, efficient, healthy (and delicious!) food, it also helps to restore and strengthen critical natural habitat. More importantly though, it affords us the chance to connect with a living, beautiful world. When we interact with that world, it transforms us into the truest, most beautiful versions of ourselves as well.

To learn more about the author, visit anaturalplace.wordpress.com

www.ingramcontent.com/pod-product-compliance
Lightning Source LLC
Chambersburg PA
CBHW060858270326
41935CB00003B/15